ANTI-CHRIST

WILLIAM STEUART McBIRNIE
B.A., B.D., M.R.E., Ph.D., F.R.G.S., Th.D., L.H.D., O.S.J.

Acclaimed Books
Dallas, Texas

Distributed by
Cross Roads Books
#3 Corporate Square
Atlanta, Georgia 30329

ii

ACCLAIMED BOOKS
P.O. Box 18186
Dallas, Texas 75218

A department of
International Prison Ministry
P.O. Box 63, Dallas, Texas 75221

Library of Congress Cataloging in Publication Data

McBirnie, William Steuart, 1920-
    Antichrist.
    1.   Antichrist.   I.   Title.
BT985.M28   236   78-14448
ISBN 0-932294-00-6

Printed in the United States of America.

All scriptural quotations from the Authorized King
James Version of the Bible, unless otherwise noted in
text.

Acclaimed Books
Dallas, Texas

Contents

Foreword

This book has a very special meaning for me because it was written by my friend and pastor, Dr. W.S. McBirnie of the United Community Church of Glendale, California.

We have traveled together into many of the lands mentioned in this book—to Persia (Iran), Turkey, Rome, Israel, Syria, Lebanon, Jordan, Egypt—and visited the places where the battles of World War III will be fought.

Dr. McBirnie has the unique ability to bring history to life so that his readers feel that they know the times, the customs and the people of other eras.

Now he has done this same thing with the future, explaining the forces behind the moving events that will soon take place as the prophecies of Daniel, Ezekiel and John the Revelator come into fulfillment.

Dr. McBirnie is an author, biblical scholar, professor at the California Graduate School of Theology, radio commentator, minister and humanitarian.

Born in Toronto, Canada, his father was a minister, his mother a concert cellist. He is an American citizen by choice, and is deeply devoted to his chosen country.

Dr. McBirnie is a graduate of the Southwestern

Baptist Theological Seminary, and moved to California in 1961 to become Senior Minister of the then newly-formed United Community Church of Glendale. Under his guidance the membership has grown to more than twelve hundred Christians from more than thirty denominations.

He has been knighted twice (Knights of Malta, Order of St. John) and was the second person to receive the Israeli Pilgrim's Medal (Pope Paul was the first recipient). Dr. McBirnie is listed in "Who's Who in the Protestant Clergy" and "Who's Who in California." He was reported by the Gallup Poll as "one of the men most admired by the American people" for 1964.

His books on various biblical and historical subjects are numerous: *The Search for the Twelve Apostles,* Tyndale House; *The Search for the Authentic Tomb of Jesus,* Acclaimed Books; *The Search for the Early Church,* Tyndale House; *How to Motivate Your Child Toward Success,* Tyndale House; *The Secret Weapons,* Acclaimed Books; *Preaching on the Life of Christ,* Zondervan; and *How to Protect Your Child,* Acclaimed Books, are only a few among the many he has written. His book on the Apostles has reached best seller status and the booklets he has authored exceed four hundred different titles.

This book was written as a project for the California Graduate School of Theology where Dr. McBirnie was professor of Middle Eastern Studies.

Chaplain Ray
International Prison Ministry
Dallas, Texas 75221

Introduction

There is a great deal of detailed information in the Bible about the world's last dictator, "the Antichrist." As far as this writer knows, no comprehensive study has until now been made of this coming great world leader which attempts to set forth all that can be known about him and which indeed *should* be known, though his nature and works are widely mentioned among those who accept the validity and relevance of biblical prophecy.

This book is intended as a thorough study of this subject.

It should be noted that there is a greater interest in the Antichrist today than ever before. The film studio, Twentieth Century-Fox, has made two major motion pictures on the Antichrist, taking biblical prophecies about him seriously for the first time in cinematic history.

In these films, the proposition that the Antichrist is already on earth today, as a child, unrecognized, but mysteriously protected by Satan, is a valid one if these indeed are the "last days" of this age. One need not agree with the story line of these films in every detail to recognize their great value in heightening public consciousness about biblical prophecy and the fact that the Antichrist, if he is to be mature enough to attempt to rule the world in the near future must, in fact, be somewhere on earth *at the present*.

The study which produced this book was used by Twentieth Century-Fox as source material for the second of these films, at this writing called *Damien—Omen II*. This motion picture depicts the Antichrist-to-be, Damien, as a teen-age boy who brings destruction upon his relatives, who have gradually realized that, in a supernatural way, the boy is dreadfully different from other boys.

This, of course, is dramatic license. The real Antichrist may or may not have this effect. While the studio intends that these two films be entertainment of the horror variety, perhaps the movies will render a valuable service to the Christian cause; millions who do not now take the idea of the Antichrist seriously, perhaps will for the first time.

This writer has been retained as the religious, technical advisor to Twentiety Century-Fox in the production of the second of the *Omen* films. The studio is attempting to present a film which entertains, yet remains consistent with the biblical portrait of the Antichrist. They have graciously made numerous adjustments in the story line as suggested by this writer.

We have attempted here a complete biblical exposition of the subject of the Antichrist. Doubtless we shall know more about the matter as time goes by. Biblical prophecy is like a distant city glimpsed at times through the mists of evening. Occasionally the mists are momentarily blown away and we see the city lights. Then the mists settle back down and obscure the road as we travel through a valley where the clouds are heavy. Yet the closer we come, the more often the lights are visible. Despite the clouds we go on, for we have seen the city!

W.S. McBirnie, Ph.D.
California Graduate School of Theology
Glendale, California

CHAPTER 1

Is The End Approaching?

In recent years there has been a revival of interest in the ancient prophecies of the Bible. Though some people scoff at the supernatural, an increasing number are beginning to believe. Why is this? The thoughtful reader should consider the following reason:

1. Man's problems have grown too great for him to solve. Perplexing difficulties, such as war and peace, the energy crisis, the population explosion, and the threat of communist-inspired world conquest by revolution, seem without a solution. Perhaps this age is indeed at last approaching its terrible end!

2. Many prophecies, previously thought impossible of fulfullment, have now, by the technology of our age, become both possible and comprehensible.

3. The conditions in our world today more closely resemble those of which Jesus spoke in His prophetic utterances than have circumstances in any other periods of history.

4.   As Bible prophecy predicts, Israel has again become a nation for the first time since shortly after the time of Jesus. This return is said by Jesus (in His parable of the fig tree) to be the foremost sign of the approaching end of this age.

5.   The alignment of hostile nations spoken of in Ezekiel 38 has at last developed: the Soviet bloc versus the Arab and Western European nations. We can now, for the first time, identify with certainty all the nations which are named by Ezekiel in the geographical designations of his day.

6.   There is today, at one time, both a religious apostasy *and* a spiritual revival. The apostates scorn biblical prophecy while those sharing in God's current spiritual renewal confirm and affirm it.

7.   Once again can be seen the visible emergence of God's spiritual "remnant." These spiritually alive people bear all the responsibility for God's work in the world at this time.

8.   The rise of modern cults has forced us to look with new attention at the prophetic Scriptures. In some instances, these false religions have fulfilled the prophecies exactly as written. Most cults in their philosophies major in the "art of living," whereas the gospel of Christ majors in the person and work of God in Christ, reconciling man unto Himself. This difference is a fulfillment of prophecy.

9.   Much new evidence has come to light to remind us that the Bible is true. Thus prophecy is more believable than ever before since it makes up a substantial part of a book which is not authenticated in many parts of archaeological discoveries.

10.   The forces and movements of the Antichrist are identifiably present in the world today as never before.

Study With Caution

Christians are called to "preach Christ," not theorize about the Antichrist. The danger of being too absorbed in studies of this kind, or any other detail of biblical prophecy, is that one may get his eyes off the Son of God and upon the son of Satan, speculating about world events to the neglect of spiritual truth. Mere knowledge of religious facts without consequent faith translated into action is closer to ancient gnosticism than to real Christianity.

There is, on the other hand, a danger of neglecting the "whole counsel of God," which certainly exhorts us to carefully watch the prophetic signs. We are not to exalt the signs of the times until they crowd out the whole gospel, but neither are we to ignore them, if we take the words of Jesus at face value:

> *"Watch ye therefore, and pray always, that ye may be accounted worthy to escape all these things that shall come to pass, and to stand before the Son of man" (Luke 21:36).*

To study responsibly the prophetic portions of the Bible with balance and a keen sense of priorities is to do what we should do. The Apostle Paul reminds us to "despise not prophesyings" (I Thess. 5:20).

Setting forth the truth about the Antichrist should not be confused with preaching the gospel. Information about the Antichrist may be true, but it is not the truth which gives life. Christ alone is the Truth, the Way and the Life. The gospel is the good news that God cares and saves. Information about the Antichrist is bad news! Any study of the Antichrist should, in the admonition of the marriage ritual, "be entered upon discreetly and in the fear of God."

The Historical Conflict

Long ago theological thinkers sensed a *dualism* at work in the world. For examples, from the Dead Sea Scrolls scholars have translated a curious writing called, *The Wars Between the Sons of Darkness and the Children of Light.* This doctrine has also been suggested in the Chinese concept of the Yin and the Yang, the excessive dualisms of the second and third-century Manicheans, and even in Genesis, where it is stated:

> *"And I will put enmity between thee (Satan) and the woman (Eve), and between thy seed (the children of Satan, including eventually the Antichrist) and her seed (the children of men and ultimately the Son of Man, Jesus); it (Jesus Christ) shall bruise thy head (conquer Satan), and thou (Satan) shall bruise his heel (cause great, though not fatal harm)" (Gen. 3:15).*

The doctrine of the coming of the Antichrist, reduced to its simplest principle is that the Antichrist is the person who embodies the dark side of this historic conflict in a satanic attempt to seize the world and maintain a successful rebellion against the Christ of God.

There have been many antichrists (men who possess some of the evil characteristics of the great Antichrist), as John tells us, ". . . ye have heard that antichrist shall come, even now are there many antichrists" (I John 2:18). Antichrists were numerous in his day and probably have been in every era since.

But this continuing spirit of rebellion and deception is to climax when Satan is finally expelled from God's bar of justice in heaven, where he continuously appears in the present time as the "accuser of the brethren." The first chapter of Job and the book of The Revelation both describe Satan's access to heaven to denounce God's people. We may be approaching his final banishment from God's presence, for even now the forces of the dark kingdom seem to be motivated by an increased malignity.

Doubtless the Antichrist is an incarnation of Satan just as Jesus Christ is the incarnation of Satan's archenemy, the living God. We do not know that Satan cannot assume bodily form, but it seems from biblical teaching that he does not. Instead he enters human beings and possesses them.

The Antichrist, as the embodiment of Satan, is a counterfeit of Christ, a morally dark messiah. He is a worker of wonders. His "miracles," whether real or illusory, are deceptive in nature. Satan's aim is to deflect the worship of mankind from God to himself and to his chosen "messiah," the Antichrist.

The rise of the occult is a manifestation of Satan's goal to prepare the nations of the world for belief in the coming false messiah. His "miracles" are intended to secure faith in his supernatural abilities.

Men will always have some religious beliefs, but if they turn from the true God to a deceiver, their "faith" will prove their ultimate downfall. Thus false religion is always the enemy of the true. The worst of all false religions will be belief in the Antichrist. We should not, therefore, expect religion or the "religious" spirit in man to wane in these last days, but rather to remain or even increase. That very spirit will be a deceptive tool in the hands of Satan.

Look For His Footprints

Since antichrists have always existed, we cannot

be too dogmatic in affirming that the coming of the supreme and ultimate antichrist is near. Yet a number of new developments, more now than at any other single time in history, may well indicate the Antichrist himself is now alive, though as yet unrevealed.

Unfortunately, little fresh research is being done on the subject of the Antichrist, if one is to judge from the scarcity of recent publications. There are dangers in the neglect of so important an issue. *The Antichrist may soon appear and be recognized.* This happened to Jesus Christ, and it is possible that Satan would dearly love to counterfeit even this.

The Christian world may be guilty of accepting without question the conclusions of recent, less-informed generations of respected biblical and prophetic scholars. Their conclusions may or may not be correct. But when writings continue unquestioned, they assume the character of sacred traditions when, in fact, they may be erroneous or at least incomplete.

Perhaps the most important of these unwarranted conclusions, indeed, a myth, is that the Antichrist will not be known before Jesus Christ returns to resurrect the bodies of His own people, translate the living, true Christians, and conduct the judgment of the believers at the *bema* or judgment seat. This return of Christ for His own is the first stage of His Second Coming. Later he will come to reveal Himself to the whole world at the battle of Armageddon. With great dogmatism, Christians are assured by some teachers that no living believer will ever know the Antichrist before the second coming of Jesus.

Why is this belief so widespread? Jesus said there would be many clear, visible signs of His return. Perhaps it is easier to retreat from the plain statements of Scripture into an anti-intellectual, often passionate (but irresponsible) position which contends that, since, "no man knows the day or hour" of the Second Coming, then it follows that Christ can return at any time. We should be careful to distinguish between the imperatives of believing in His coming "at such an hour as ye think not" and the clear statements that certain events must precede the Second Coming. The two concepts are not incompatible as some evangelicals commonly assume.

If the Antichrist will or could appear before the first stage of Christ's second advent, it is essential we should study all Scripture about him very carefully, then look around us for his footprints. Otherwise, it would not be very important that Bible-believing Christians be concerned about the Antichrist.

That is the crux of the argument. And dogmatism either way can be dangerous.

There is another difficulty we must face: the frequent attempts to identify the Antichrist in the historical past. For example, though all Christians owe a debt to Martin Luther that cannot be quickly calculated, he did not have perfect understanding in all matters of faith.

His closed views of the Millenium and his obviously incorrect identification of the Roman Catholic pontiff as *the* Antichrist have paralyzed the willingness of many Lutheran Christians today to re-examine the entire doctrine of the Second Coming in light of contemporary knowledge, which is certainly superior to Luther's.

Equally mistaken identifications of various dictators of the past as the Antichrist have made many thoughtful Bible scholars very reluctant to even raise the issue. Hitler, Mussolini, Napoleon, Stalin, and for that matter, Alaric the Goth, Attilla the Hun, various Caesars and others have at times been called "the Antichrist." They certainly may have been antichrists, but it is obvious they were not *the* Antichrist.

Is it self-importance which causes people to dogmatically identify the Antichrist as someone who appears sufficiently dangerous and who is contemporary with them?

Do we too hold the conceit that ours is the age toward which all ages have been pointing? If so, may this not be merely unwarranted, alarmist thinking unbefitting sensible Christians? Our age, merely because it is ours, is not a candidate for the fulfillment of prophecy.

However, objectively considered, it seems that we have indeed come to that day.

The study which follows is not an attempt to identify anyone as the Antichrist. It is, however, a modest reexamination of Scripture in light of what we can now see, standing gratefully on the shoulders of all who have wrestled with this problem before. We see a few new facts, and perhaps note some errors in past conclusions. We hope to correct our trajectory before impact.

What Is He Like?

"Who is like unto the beast!" (Rev. 13:4) the multitudes of earth will exclaim. After a long period of great famines, wars and mounting problems, the one man who will seem to offer workable solutions will be hailed as a savior. But he will be a false savior. Satan's solutions, offered so glibly, frequently and often, seem to make sense—at first. In the long run, however, they lead only to deeper and more permanent misery.

The children of his kingdom who behave like their father, Satan, only *profess* to care for the welfare of man. In actuality, Satan seeks only to gain recruits in his long war against God. In the end he will sacrifice them mercilessly.

The Antichrist has "eyes like the eyes of man" (Dan. 7:8), thus signifying that he seems like a man, even though a superior one. Yet he is strangely diverse from those who precede him (Dan. 7:7).

But he is more than human because he is empowered by Satan, ascending to his position of leadership through satanic assistance (Rev. 13:2). He is called the "son of perdition" (II Thess. 2:3).

An orator (Dan. 7:8), he speaks with enormous presence and influence (i.e., Rev. 13:2), "the mouth of a lion"). The content of his words relates to "great things" (Rev. 13:5), but in the end leads to blasphemy (Rev. 13:5).

The Antichrist may be a philosopher, for he understands "dark sentences" (Dan. 8:23). He will deal with the occult (Rev. 16:13, 14) and will rationalize the truth of God, turn it into a lie (I John 4:1-6) and deceive many. In fact he will use religion (Rev. 13:4) for his own purposes. At first he will seem to provide people a relief from the secularism and godlessness of this age, but "in their security will corrupt many" (Dan. 8:25 RSV).

In appearance he is described as one "whose look was more stout than his fellows" (Dan. 7:20). He is also called a "king of fierce countenance" (Dan. 8:23). By dramatizing his acts and words through public display (II Thess. 2:4), he will attract multitudes of adoring, worshiping followers (Rev. 13:3, 4; 17:8).

He will be a military genius (Dan. 7:24: Rev. 13:4) and a politician of unusual wiliness and craftiness (Dan. 8:25). Selfish ambition will rule his every move, for "he shall exalt himself, and magnify himself above every god. . . Neither shall he regard the God of his fathers, nor the desire of women, nor regard (personally) any god; for he shall magnify himself above all" (Dan. 11:36, 37).

These then are the characteristics of the "man of sin," the "lawless one" (II Thess. 2:8). Why would the Bible go to such lengths to describe this man in so much detail if Christians in the "end time" were not to look for him?

Those left on earth who belatedly come to Christ after Christ's return for His people would hardly need so much detail because the Antichrist will be very much in evidence. Indeed, they can hardly ignore or mistake him because he will be conspicuously the most important man in the entire world.

Most assuredly, he will not be revealed to the majority of the public before Christ returns for His own. But those who understand spiritual things may very well be able to detect his presence just before the Lord's return.

Obviously, the Antichrist will have to be on earth before the return of Christ for His people, for he will be mature enough to rule the world for at least three and a half years after the first return of Christ, the "parousia."

We cannot be dogmatic about the precise date of Christ's return, but it is unquestionable that certain world conditions will prevail and make way for the Antichrist—some which are present; others which do not yet prevail. In brief, the second coming of Jesus

Christ and the appearance on earth of the Antichrist will coincide. To look for the coming of the Antichrist is also to look for the signs of the coming again of Jesus Christ. We cannot separate one from the other. This is why it is so important to examine all that can be known about the Antichrist's appearance.

CHAPTER 2

The Master's Warning

We dare not proceed in an exhaustive study of the Antichrist without first reflecting on what Jesus said to His disciples about this man. As Satan is the greatest created being in power, personality and attributes, so the Antichrist will be a man of great capacity, perhaps the most gifted man who ever lived. No ordinary human would be chosen to be Satan's emissary. To the Antichrist's natural gifts, which have already been described in the first chapter of this study, will be added Satan's throne, power and great authority (Rev. 13:2).

This distinctive combination of natural capacities and satanic power will make the Antichrist a person who can persuade men to accept him as the authentic Messiah. He will go to great pains to imitate certain superficial traits of the real Messiah, but he will be a messiah of evil rather than of good.

Inasmuch as the real author of the book of The Revelation is not John but Jesus Christ (Rev. 1:1), all that is given to us in that book concerning the Antichrist can be said to be what Jesus said about him. But we shall leave the insights of the book of The Revelation to a later study and restrict this chapter to what is written and quoted from Jesus in other books of the New Testament.

John's Record

Prior to writing his first epistle, John must have quoted to his readers the teaching of Jesus concerning the Antichrist, for he writes, "Little children, it is the last time: and *as ye have heard* that antichrist shall come. . ." (I John 2:18). The evidence here is surely indicative that what John wrote about the Antichrist is what he had heard from Jesus Himself and had already taught his flock at Ephesus.

It is not enough to merely draw the conclusion that Jesus told John, and probably the other disciples, about the Antichrist. What in particular can we conclude or deduce from John's statements as to what Jesus Himself is recorded to have said?

1. First, we see there is to be a person who is given the title "Antichrist." If we did not learn it from John, we would not have this particular name, because "Antichrist" appears only in the writings of John. Other designations for the Antichrist are used in other books. John, who was closest to Jesus, must have heard this name from Jesus.

2. The Antichrist is to be associated with the "last days." John said the appearance of many antichrists demonstrated the fact that his generation was in the "last time" (I John 2:18). There is an escatalogical problem here.

How could John's century and (possibly) our own both be called "the last time?" Perhaps in light of the great sweep of history, the entire last 1,900 years are to be thought of as the "last time." This is frankly a mystery we cannot solve. It is quite evident that the supreme Antichrist did not appear during John's day or soon thereafter. For that matter, the final Antichrist has not yet appeared.

Perhaps we shall someday solve this mystery, but not from present knowledge. We must be content with the assurance of the general teaching of the New Testament that the doom of the Antichrist will be accomplished only at the time of Christ's return. Paul was careful to tell us in II Thessalonians 2:2, 3 that the first stage of the Lord's coming will not occur "until the man of sin be revealed, the son of perdition."

All we can conclude at this point, therefore, is that the period associated with the end of the "last times" is the time of the real Antichrist.

3.   John also states that the coming of the great Antichrist will be associataed with the appearance of many antichrists. This was factually true in the emperor-worshiping Roman Empire, but it has also been true at times since. As we shall see, Jesus affirmed that this would also be the case in the last days of the "end times."

4.   John also pointed out that all those whom he calls "antichrists" can be identified as those who deny the incarnation of Jesus Christ (II John 7). Certainly an "antichrist," and most particularly *the* Antichrist, will not admit that Jesus was the incarnate Son of God, the true Messiah. Their counterfeiting natures as false Christs forbids their tribute to the true Christ. Of this we can be certain.

The Gospel Account

Jesus doubtless referred to the Antichrist when, as John records in John 5:43, He spoke of him as "one who would come in his own name." This may mean the Antichrist will not claim any authority from the true God for his own work, yet he will probably not admit openly that he is of Satan, which he is. It is logical to conclude he will come as a "self-made man," certainly a part of his deception.

As Jesus sat on the Mount of Olives after His triumphal entry into Jerusalem, his disciples began to question Him about the signs of His coming and the end of the age. He set forth the following teaching concerning the last days, false Christs and the Antichrist, whom He called "the abomination of desolation:"

> *"And Jesus answered and said unto them, Take heed that no man deceive you. For many shall come in my name, saying I am Christ; and shall deceive many (Matt. 24:4,5).*

> *"When ye therefore shall see the abomination of desolation, spoken of by Daniel the prophet, stand in the holy place, (Whoso readeth, let him understand:) Then let them which be in Judaea flee into the mountains" (Matt. 24:15, 16).*

> *"Then there shall be great tribulation" (Matt. 24:21).*

> *"Then if any man shall say unto you, Lo, here is Christ, or there; believe it not. For there shall arise false Christs, and false prophets, and shall shew great signs and wonders; insomuch that, if it were possible, they shall deceive the very elect" (Matt. 24:23-24).*

> *"Wherefore if they shall say unto you, Be-*

hold, he is in the desert; go not forth: behold, he is in the secret chambers; believe it not" (Matt. 24:26).

"And then shall appear the sign of the Son of man in heaven: and then shall all the tribes of the earth mourn, and they shall see the Son of man coming in the clouds of heaven with power and great glory" (Matt. 24:30).

"Who then is a faithful and wise servant, whom his Lord hath made ruler over his household, to give them meat in due season?" (Matt. 24:45).

From these statements we may draw these conclusions:

1. Down through the ages, there have been many false messiahs, or "antichrists." Their claims to "Christhood" is a denial of the true Christ.

2. One false Christ (messiah) will be greater than others. The operative phrase or title, "the abomination of desolation," simply means, "the abominable person who lays waste or desolates the land," that is, the destroyer (Antichrist) who is disgusting or abominable in the sight of God and His people.

3. The supreme Antichrist will come to Jerusalem to the holy Temple. This implies clearly that the Temple shall have by that time been constructed!

4. The supreme Antichrist will persecute God's people who are then alive. Those who live in Judaea are urged to flee in great haste when they see him in Jerusalem (Matt. 24:16).

5. For a fuller explanation of the Antichrist and his work, Jesus refers his listeners to the book of Daniel (Matt. 24:15). Incidentally, in doing so, Jesus

affirmed the inspiration and authority of the book of Daniel.

6. The great period of trouble predicted by Daniel (the Tribulation) will some day come to pass as the direct work of the Antichrist and Satan, plus the judgments and punishments of God upon a sinful world. (Matt. 24:21).

7. Believers in Jesus Christ are to disregard the claims of all other "Christs," no matter the evidence of their miracles or the witness of their advocates (Matt. 24:23). It is possible by the use of modern technology to produce the appearance of the miraculous.

8. False Christs will deceive many, except for those who have chosen the true Christ in the darkness of the Tribulation (Matt. 24:24).

9. The Antichrist is not to be mistaken for the true Christ, no matter how his advocates offer what they will call "new interpretations" of the coming of the Messiah.

He will not be in the desert, in secret rooms or incognito. Christ Himself shall ultimately come in one way only—openly and publicly at the Battle of Armageddon in the second stage of His Second Coming (Matt. 24:30, 31).

10. The Antichrist will "prove" he is the world's looked-for "messiah" by his wars, miracles and false assertions, all designed to deceive. The true Christ will come (at the first stage of His second coming) to remove His own people. Later He will come to conquer His enemies (Matt. 24:30, 31).

11. The wise servant of God will feed the people with the truth (in context, the truth about the Antichrist) until the Lord returns. The phrase used is,

"give them their meat in due season (Matt. 24:45), or
"issue their balanced rations at the proper time."

Not For Christ's Day

It is instructive to note that in the first century
Jesus referred to the Antichrist as *yet to come.*
Therefore, the prophecies of Daniel about the Antichrist are, according to Jesus, for the future, not the
time of Antiochus Epiphanes, a Greek general who,
long before Christ, persecuted the Jews and blasphemously sacrificed a hog on the altar of the Temple
in Jerusalem. Antiochus was an evil blasphemer and
persecutor supposed by many to have fulfilled
Daniel's predictions. This conclusion is unwarranted. The Antichrist is yet to come, and he is to be
destroyed by the return of Christ at Armageddon.

It is also an unmistakable truth that Jesus did not
say much that was new about the Antichrist apart
from that which was generally known to anyone who
could read the existing book of Daniel. This lends
enormous prestige to the book of Daniel and is a
witness to its historicity and accuracy.

In effect, Jesus was saying, "Learn about the
Antichrist from the book of Daniel. I will add only
what my people are to know and do when the
Antichrist appears. Above all, they are not to be
deceived, for the Antichrist is doomed. He is a false
messiah who will deceive all but God's elect. I will
bring this false messiah down and spare many.
Watch for him and other things which are to happen
at the time of My coming so nothing will take you by
surprise."

CHAPTER 3

Will The Antichrist Please Stand

Inasmuch as the Antichrist will not be revealed to the world at large before the first stage of Christ's second coming, it has been widely assumed that he could not be alive in the world today. This is not necessarily true for three reasons:

1. When the Antichrist is revealed, and even before he comes to power, he must already be a mature man, capable of acquiring and using political power. This would open the possibility that he could now be on earth as a child, a young man, or even a mature man.

2. If the days of the present mark the period of the end time, they are most assuredly the days for the fulfillment of much prophecy. "This generation shall not pass, till all be fulfilled," Jesus said in Matthew 24:34. Which generation? The one which sees the beginning of the fulfillment of latter-day prophecy will generally still be alive to see the end of it. Therefore, if our generation is indeed the final one of

this age, it is reasonable to conclude that somewhere the Antichrist is already in existence, though unknown.

3. The world-at-large may not recognize the Antichrist until he reveals himself immediately following the first stage of the Second Coming, though there is no scriptural reason why Christians taught in the Word of God should not be able to recognize and identify him long before the Lord returns. About end-time prophecy, Daniel recorded, "None of the wicked shall understand; but the wise shall understand" (Dan. 12:10).

We should thus address ourselves to the study of conditions which produce the Antichrist, or more accurately, to the circumstances from which he will emerge.

One of the foremost, present-day authorities on Bible prophecy, Dr. S.I. McMillen, has a cogent word for us on the emergence of the Antichrist from the Soviet Union:

> "If any unprejudiced person would study only Daniel's portrait of the Antichrist, he should readily identify that tyrant when he appears on the world's stage.
>
> "One should keep the main features of Daniel's portrait in mind. With these he should keep seeking to identify the nation most likely to produce this future ruler. Here are the chief distinctives:
>
> > "1. He may emerge from a country within the bounds of the ancient Grecian Empire (Dan. 8:9), a part of it at least.
> > "2. His ideology is different from the preceding nations (Dan. 7:24).

"3. He can be recognized by his blatant defiance of God and his persecution of God's followers (Dan. 7:25).

"4. He has 'great shrewdness and intelligence' and is skilled in intrigues (Dan. 8:23).

"5. He is characterized by his takeover of other nations (Dan. 7:24).

"6. He is nihilistic—destroys 'all laws, morals and customs' (Dan. 7:25). Russia originated nihilism in the nineteenth century.

"7. The time of his appearance is dated: 'the last days' or 'that final event in history' (Dan. 8:17, 19; 12:4, 9, 13).

"8. The length of his persecution of Israel is repeatedly given as three and a half years (Dan. 7:25; 9:27; 12:7).

"One must ever keep all of his ideas about the Antichrist fluid. His thinking must never petrify." (S.I. McMillen, *Discern These Times*)

We have quoted Dr. McMillen at length to demonstrate evidence which should help identify the Antichrist someday. It is this writer's opinion, however, that the Antichrist will arise from the chaos and power balance vacuum following the defeat of the Russian-led forces, which according to Ezekiel 38, will invade the Middle East and be destroyed. If so, the Antichrist may arise from some smaller nation which was once part of the Greek and Roman empires rather than from the Soviet Union.

His Origins

The "Beast" has certain characteristics which will focus the attention of informed Christians upon him before he reveals himself to the world as the Antichrist.

1. His Geographical Area

The area from which the Antichrist comes was ruled by both Roman and Greek empires. Ten nations are indicated by Daniel. These can be identified with the makeup of the Roman Empire under Domitian.

> *"Therefore the he goat waxed very great: and when he was strong, the great horn (Alexander the Great) was broken ('horn' in Scripture refers to power or kingdom); and for it came up four notable ones (i.e., Alexander's successors) toward the four winds of heaven. And out on one of them (i.e., one of the divisions of the Greek Empire, which in Alexander's day included a part of what is today the USSR) came forth a little horn (the Antichrist), which waxed exceeding great, toward the south, and toward the east, and toward the pleasant land (i.e., the Holy Land)" (Dan. 8:8, 9).*

The book of The Revelation speaks of the consolidation of a ten-nation confederacy in the latter days. Many have wondered if this would be the same as the area of the Common Market? This is possible. The only movement on earth today which bears every characteristaic of the Antichrist is that of Eastern Europe, which is not likely to be admitted to the Common Market. Nevertheless, when Europe unites —as it someday must, to become a third-world power for its own survival—it will provide the ideal stage for the emergence of the Antichrist.

Both the Soviet Union and several other nations

now in the Eastern Europe communist bloc were also incorporated in the ancient Roman Empire. They include Rumania, Yugoslavia, Bulgaria, Czechoslovakia, Armenia and parts of East Germany.

Could the Antichrist come from Rome? This is possible. Since, however, he is to destroy the city mystically called "Babylon" (Rev. 14:8; 17:5), which in The Revelation is presumably a symbolic word for apostate Rome, it does not seem likely that he himself would be a native of Rome. We cannot, however, entirely overlook Italy as a possible birthplace for the Antichrist, since it has an enormous Communist Party which could in the future prove a threat to a Europe attempting to unite following the destruction of the Soviet Union. This result seems the only possible outcome of the battle described in Ezekiel 38 and 39.

2. His Racial Origin

Many think the Antichrist will be a Jew, since he will attempt to achieve recognition by the Jews as their Messiah. This theory cannot be ruled out, but there is little scriptural evidence to back it up.

Not all Jews live in Israel. Many atheistic Jews live in communist countries and elsewhere, and some are even Communists. Perhaps in this sense, the Antichrist could well be a Jew by race. But this is only an opinion and is not derived from a specific, scriptural reference.

What we do know about him is:

> "Neither shall he regard the God of his fathers, nor the desire of women, nor regard any god: for he shall magnify himself above all" (Dan. 11:37).

This denial of the "God of his fathers" indicates

that the people from whom he comes are worshipers
of the true God rather than a pagan people. Hence his
ancestors could be Christians or Jews.

This verse also suggests the distinct possibility that
the Antichrist may be a homosexual (he will not
regard "the desire of women"). Could the increase of
homosexuality in our day be a part of the con-
ditioning of the world for the Antichrist? It may well
be.

3. His Spiritual Origin

He is to be the seed (child) of the serpent (Gen.
3:15). He is described as ascending out of the
bottomless pit, but this need imply only that, as the
Antichrist, he will be of Satan and demon-possessed
(Rev. 11:7; 17:8).

4. His Political Origin

He will appear first as one among several political
leaders, but afterwards will grow in influence. Initially he is a "little horn" (meaning having little
power"), starting with an insignificant number of
people: "I considered the horns, and, behold, there
came up among them another little horn" (Dan. 7:8).
This seems to preclude his arising from the Soviet
Union.

Eventually, he will become strong by statesmanship. "He shall be diverse from the first (king), and *he
shall subdue three kings*"(Dan. 7:24).

The whole biblical teaching about the Antichrist
demonstrates that he is a lying, crafty, oratorical
politician who is ruthless, treacherous and bloody.
Most Communist leaders have these characteristics.
Nevertheless, it is not absolutely certain that the
Antichrist will be a communist in the Marxist-
Leninist sense, only that he will be a dictator who

uses many communist methods. It may well be that he will be an anti-communist who will promise to rid the world of the threat of communism.

5. His Social Origin

The Antichrist must arise out of social chaos. This may be in part due, firstly, to the shattering of the Soviet-led confederation occurring as a result of the defeat of its armies in the invasion of Israel (Ezek. 38); and, secondly, to the "fire upon Magog" mentioned in Ezekiel 38-39. He will be initially an anarchist, since he is the arch-destroyer (Rev. 13). At this stage of our knowledge, it would seem that he is to be, or would profess to be, the personalization of the answer to the threat of communism.

In Luke, Jesus describes the conditions of social chaos which will prevail in the environment of this supreme opportunist:

> *"And there shall be signs in the sun, and in the moon, and in the stars, and upon the earth distress of nations, with perplexity; the sea and the waves roaring; Men's hearts failing them for fear, and for looking after those things which are coming on the earth; for the powers of heaven shall be shaken" (Luke 21:16).*

Christians must oppose all anarchy because it is certain to be the initial method of the Antichrist. If we are to hold him at bay for a time, anarchy (planned social chaos aimed at destroying public confidence in the power of their government to protect them) must be kept minimal.

6. His Religious Origin

Although the Antichrist will be an atheist, he will ally himself with the "False Prophet" who will head

the apostate religion of the last days. The trend
toward an alliance combining various religious
groups is already present and growing. This is seen in
(1) an increasing friendliness of apostate Christianity
with the extreme left; (2) the World Council of
Churches' (WCC) current gifts to Communist revo-
lutionists; and (3) the refusal of the WCC to con-
demn communism. These acts are cases in point
which demonstrate a potential unity between certain
types of socialist-minded religious leaders and the
person who is to be the Antichrist. If this is so, we
shall see religious leaders who today are pro-communists become anti-communists as a reaction to
Soviet imperialism and its responsibility for World
War III. Such a switch in attitude was seen once
before, at the start of World War II, as a consequence of the Hitler-Stalin pact. The fluctuation of
loyalties caused a setback in the communist movement during World War II.

While clues to the origins of the Antichrist do not
provide an unmistakable guide to any certain man
now living, the near future may confirm many of
these characteristics in a surfacing political leader.
Christians who master the particulars about him may
soon see him suddenly and surprisingly emerge.

In these last days of the age, there is no room to
doubt that somewhere the man who is to be the
Antichrist is now alive, perhaps already plotting the
greatest power-grab in history.

As Jesus was on earth thirty years before He was
revealed as the Christ, so also might the Antichrist
copy Jesus even in this.

CHAPTER 4

Deceived!

How will the Antichrist arise? Why will people hail his emergence? Simply because the world and mankind are even now being prepared for him.

The Antichrist will receive his supernatural power from Satan, and hence will be a product of diabolical genius. He will seize the opportunity to destroy things as they are and rise to the power which is presented during certain chaotic social conditions. Most dictators have come to power by similar means.

As great as the Antichrist's natural gifts will be, and as great as his power from Satan will be, Satan, the master strategist, will yet need to carefully prepare mankind for the advent of his Antichrist. Even Satan cannot maneuver people instantly.

Jesus came forth "in the fullness of time" to a world scene long prepared for Him. The religious life of ancient Israel, the ministry of John the Baptist, the Roman government and roads, the Greek culture, language and philosophy, the exploration and open-

ing of a world wider than had been known before—all
these conditions helped set the stage for Jesus to
present Himself as Messiah and Savior.

Preconditioning Movements

If Christianity is not constantly renewed by con-
versions, and the churches strengthened until the day
Jesus returns, the light of the gospel could be snuffed
out even in America.

We can see examples in Red China and Albania,
communist-dominated countries which have closed
the churches. God forbid that we should have to
prematurely live under a communist dictatorship
because of our failure to resist it. It is just about as
bad to live in a communist-dominated society as to
live in a society governed by the Antichrist.

Movements such as communism are the results of
the "spirit of antichrist" and are the forerunners of
the Beast's future complete victories. They are on
hand today, spreading and preparing the minds of
unregenerate men for surrender to the Antichrist.
This will occur when the hindering or restraining
power of Christians, churches and the Holy Spirit are
removed at the moment of Christ's return.

*"For the mystery of iniquity doth already
work: only he who now letteth (hindereth) will
let (hinder), until he be taken out of the way. And
then shall that Wicked be revealed" (II Thess.
2:7-8).*

● Religious movements which prepare the world for
the Antichrist are clearly visible in our times. There
are two broad classifications of anti-Christian religions:

1. Paganism or idolatry which can be easily turned to the worship of the image of the the Beast. What is one more idol to a pagan?

"And the third angel followed them, saying with a loud voice, If any man worship the beast and his image, and receive his mark in his forehead or in his hand, The same shall drink of the wine of the wrath of God" (Rev. 14:9, 10).

2. Apostasy and heresy, which are not the same, but similar, will arise. Heresy is to depart from the full truth of the "faith once delivered" by adding to it, while apostasy is to depart from the faith by taking away from it. Heresy believes more than orthodoxy, while apostasy believes less. But both are essentially the product of pride, and hence are not of God.

Both apostasy and heresy (if serious enough) prepare people for the Antichrist because they corrupt or deny the faith of Christ and are products of Satan who would corrupt or weaken the gospel.

John gives us an example:

"And every spirit that confesseth not that Jesus Christ is come in the flesh is not of God: and this is that spirit of antichrist" (I John 4:3).

The Christians should have nothing to do with either heresy or apostasy, but rather be active in a church which proclaims the historic Christian gospel and opposes the spirit of Antichrist.

3. Political movements, which prepare the world for the coming political kingdom of the Antichrist, are easy to see today, and are characterized by their opposition to Christ and a biblical view of man and society.

The Antichrist will have these political characteristics: He will be a godless materialist, honoring only "the god of forces (war)." He will subscribe to Mao Tse-tung's dictum, "Political power comes from the mouth of the gun." Thus the Antichrist will be some kind of fascist-socialist dictator under whom the power of the state is absolute.

He will control all commerce, hence he will be a socialist who seizes and manipulates the means of production and distribution. His government shall decree "that no man might buy or sell, save he that had the mark, or the name of the beast, or the number of his name" (Rev. 13:17).

In addition, the Antichrist will be a master military strategist, seizing all weapons and enlisting a great army to enforce his will. He is the embodiment of dictatorship, communism, socialism, anarchy, fascism and materialism. No Christian should encourage any of these through an acceptance of their deceptive humanitarianism, godless, doctrinal or political theories!

4. Immoral movements which prepare the world for the Antichrist by weakening or silencing the claims of God and His absolute moral law are products of the spirit of Antichrist. They are now effectively organized and commercialized, and are considered respectable in many places.

Saint Paul observed this in his second epistle to Timothy. Note the characteristics of evil men listed in the first few verses of chapter 3:

> *"This know also, that in the last days perilous times shall come. "For men shall be lovers of their own selves, covetous, boasters, proud, blasphemers, disobedient to parents, unthankful, unholy, without natural affection, truce-*

> *breakers, false accusers, incontinent, fierce, despisers of those that are good, traitors, heady, highminded, lovers of pleasures more than lovers of God" (II Tim. 3:1-4).*
>
> *"But evil men and seducers shall wax worse and worse, deceiving and being deceived" (II Tim. 3:13).*

This ugly list of sins, so characteristic of our time, is widely reflected in magazines, movies, television, the filthy "underground press," and the "new" sexual morality. It is evidenced in the breakdown of the family unit and the rise of traitors who today go unpunished in a lax and permissive society.

Also this list of characteristic sins of the last days can be seen especially in the rise of "hedonism," the devotion to pleasure so currently popular.

Superstition is also part of the "spirit of Antichrist." When men refuse God, they turn to substitutes for Him. How revealing of the spiritual bankruptcy of our so-called scientific age—in which educated mankind should have rid itself of the darkness and anti-intellectualism of superstition—that we see an astonishing revival of belief in the dark side of the supernatural.

Astrology, witchcraft, spiritualism and occultism are but a few of the superstitions and anti-Christian beliefs held by vast numbers of people today. The greatest superstition of all, however, will be the belief that the Antichrist should be worshiped, though he is but a man. All modern superstition leads toward the ready acceptance of the Antichrist by those who refuse Christ!

His "miracles" are to be like those of witches and fortunetellers today, only on a global scale with more showmanship and a vastly more evil effect.

5. The use of drugs of an overpowering nature is part of the spirit of Antichrist. It is sigificant to note that the Antichrist will take advantage of the widespread use of drugs. "For by thy sorceries were all nations deceived" (Rev. 18:23). The word "sorceries" in the original Greek means "to enchant with drugs." It is from the Greek word "pharmakia," which is related to "pharmacy" and "drugs."

This verse says the source of drugs for enchantment will be the government monopoly of the Antichrist, or at least of the False Prophet, his cohort. He promotes the world's last great movement of superstition under drug control which will be aimed at directing the world to worship the Beast, a mere man empowered by Satan.

Order of the Day

Since the five "movements" which the Antichrist will use when he is in power are already characteristic of our times and are growing with dismaying rapidity, we may conclude that the Antichrist is near at hand. The world is already being prepared for him.

If one wishes to see how rapidly this preparation is taking place, consider how most, if not all, of these movements were either not known or not very strong at the beginning of this century. Now they are everywhere present. Fifty percent of America's crime bill is necessary because of drug abuse. Church councils are riddled with pro-communists. Immorality is the hallmark of the new sexuality. Communism and dictatorship are on the rise. Socialism is rotting the character and initiative of our nation and others. Superstition abounds; pleasure is the order of the day. All of these are signs of the Antichrist.

Yes! The spirit of antichrist is here. True Christians need to clearly and firmly oppose all these movements, for why should we help those who are the enemies of the Lord?

The Antichrist will come to a world that is prepared for him. We should note that preparation, and upon the highest principles, oppose it. Christians are not required to defeat the Antichrist, but we are required to do at least four things to oppose him:

1.   We are to bear witness against the Antichrist in this age, so that after the parousia (the first stage of the Second Coming when true Christians are caught away), many others will eventually become believers, even if belatedly.

2.   We are to refuse to become a party to the present-day movements of Antichrist, lest Christians inadvertently assist his rise to power.

3.   We are to work the works of God while it is day, for "the night cometh, when no man can work" (John 9:4). Christians today should work for freedom, the salvation of souls and the Church.

4.   We are to do everything possible to actively resist the movements of Antichrist, so that, if possible, his kingdom may be delayed. This delay would allow more time for people to be brought into the family of God to consequently join churches which faithfully oppose the Antichrist.

CHAPTER 5

The Forerunners

John the Baptist was the forerunner of Jesus
Christ.

> *"In those days came John the Baptist, preach-*
> *ing in the wilderness of Judaea, And saying,*
> *Repent ye: for the kingdom of heaven is at hand.*
> *For this is he that was spoken of by the prophet*
> *Esaias, saying, The voice of one crying in the*
> *wilderness, Prepare ye the way of the Lord,*
> *make his paths straight" (Matt. 3:1-3).*

John's role was to heighten the spiritual consciousness of Israel and create anticipation for the
coming of Jesus.

Compare the following verse of prophecy concerning the ministry of John the Baptist. The first is the
closing two verses of the Old Testament:

> *"Behold, I will send you Elijah the prophet*
> *before the coming of the great and dreadful day*
> *of the Lord: And he shall turn the heart of the*

fathers to the children, and the heart of the children to their fathers" (Mal. 4:5, 6).

The second is from Jesus in the New Testament:

"For this is he, of whom it is written, Behold, I send my messenger before thy face, which shall prepare thy way before thee" (Matt. 11:10).

"And if ye receive it, this is Elias, which was for to come (Matt. 11:14).

"Then the disciples understood that he spake unto them of John the Baptist" (Matt. 17:13).

"And he (John the Baptist) shall go before him (Jesus) in the spirit and power of Elias: . . . to make ready a people prepared for the Lord" (Luke 1:17).

Thus we see that as John the Baptist came in the spirit (attitude) of Elijah (spelled Elias in the New Testament) so also will counterparts and forerunners come in the "spirit" or attitude of the great Antichrist.

These forerunners, people and movements, will help Satan dull the spiritual consciousness of mankind and create blindness toward the emergence and appearance of the Antichrist.

What is to determine whether a person is an "antichrist" or not? The actions and attitudes of the person himself and the tests of Scripture are clear:

1. An antichrist is deceptive:

"For such are false apostles, deceitful workers, transforming themselves into the apostles of Christ" (II Cor. 11:13).

2. An antichrist opposes Jesus, denies Him as the historical Messiah, and refutes His incarnation:

"Who is a liar but he that denieth that Jesus is the Christ? He is antichrist, that denieth the Father and the Son" (I John 2:22).

3. An antichrist denies the second coming of Jesus Christ:

"For many deceivers are entered into the world, who confess not that Jesus Christ is coming in the flesh. This is a deceiver and an antichrist" (II John 7).

(The verb in II John 7 is present tense and is best translated into English by the expression "is coming." Thus, this verse is a reference to the second coming of Jesus.)

4. Many antichrists claim to be the divine Messiah:

"For many shall come in my name, saying, I am Christ (messiah); and shall deceive many" (Matt. 24:5).

"For there shall arise false Christs, and false prophets, and shall show great signs and wonders" (Matt. 24:24).

5. Those who are antichrists encourage people to depart from moral standards. II Timothy records the characteristics of these people in the last days. Check them once again in chapter four of this study.

Today's society is saturated with pornography, violence, immorality and outright hatred against the doers of good. Those who seek to teach or preach righteousness are mocked and threatened.

6. Those who are antichrists make religion a mere form (having vestments, ceremonies, vocabularies and titles as ministers or religious leaders, but

who are not personally surrendered to Christ). Paul warned about them:

> *"Having a form of godliness, but denying the power thereof" (II Tim. 3:5).*

7. There are antichrists who deceive in matters of religion and ideology. They discredit the true faith and cause people to trust in utterly false superstitions or substitutes of the gospel. Their philosophies are based on the so-called "art of living," which mask themselves as religions, but are in fact non-theological.

> *"But evil men and seducers shall wax worse and worse, deceiving, and being deceived" (II Tim. 3:13).*

The forerunners of the great Antichrist will share these main characteristics and possibly others as well. Their very actions tend to break down the dependence and trust in present forms of society. Satanism and the occult are on the rise. World government schemes are increasingly popular among those who do not see where this tendency will lead. Scorn of the real Messiah and opposition to Him are growing.

Antichrists of History

Various historical figures have in the past exhibited certain characteristics of the Antichrist. It is important that attention be given to anyone who has in any measure the characteristics of the great Antichrist to come. Examples in modern times abound:

Lenin, who combined the use of terror, assassination (liquidation of all opposition), atheism and obedience to Communist doctrine to make communism succeed and remain in power. Lenin is literally worshiped as a savior in Russia today. School children daily chant before his image, "Lenin lived, Lenin lives, Lenin lives forever!" This false savior has taken the pattern of the Antichrist.

Stalin, who broke every treaty he ever signed (as the Antichrist will do), liquidated whole classes of people (estimated at 26,000,000), and warred against the churches in Russia. He closed most churches and reduced others to servants of the atheistic state. Under this antichrist, effective organized Christianity was almost eliminated in Russia. In this, Stalin was a forerunner of the Antichrist.

Mussolini, the "sawdust Caesar" who taught other twentieth century dictators, such as Hitler, the effective uses of military threats and the possibility of reviving former empires. This is a plan to be followed by the Antichrist. Mussolini signed a concordat with the Vatican despite his personal rejection of Christianity and his political brutality. He was not the Antichrist, but he was *an* antichrist. He said, "I would make a league with the devil himself." So will the Antichrist.

Mao Tse-Tung, whose followers distribute through the world his book of Communist theory in greater numbers than the Bible, whose image was everywhere in China, was worshiped as the only deity permitted in Red China. Here is a forerunner of the "image of the Beast."

There are many other, lesser antichrists. They abound in greater numbers today than at any other single time in history. These powerful people appear in pulpits, classrooms, as newspaper and magazine

editors, as leftist politicians, actors and revolutionaries.

Some are prominent, others are little known. All to
one degree or another resemble the Antichrist, and
they influence many people to turn away from Christ.
All are blasphemers. Many are dabblers in the dark
side of the supernatural.

A few years ago the manager of the Beatles said
about them, "They are 'antichristers.' No one real-
izes just how antichrist they are."

Below are two newspaper articles from Ireland.
The first describes an interconnected communist
web of I.R.A. involvement and the second article
pictures a typical, political "antichrist," a genuine
forerunner of the Antichrist, who seeks to make
Ireland communistic:

> *"BELFAST (UPI) — British army sources
> said Wednesday secret documents seized dur-
> ing the occupation Irish Republican Army
> strongholds in Belfast and Londonderry dis-
> closed a wide-range of contact with guerilla,
> anarchist and other revolutionary groups
> abroad, including American Black Panthers.*

> *"British soldiers who moved into the Roman
> Catholic 'no-go' area Monday found most of the
> I.R.A. leaders and their weapons gone. But they
> uncovered a rich haul of secret papers showing
> how wide the I.R.A. has cast its net abroad, the
> source said.*

> *"The contacts included revolutionary groups
> in Cuba, North America, France, Holland,
> Belgium, Scandinavia and the Middle East.*

> *"Army intelligence has known for some time
> both official and provisional wings of the I.R.A.
> were in contact with other left-wing groups, but*

*not on the scale found in the deserted house in
Belfast, the sources said.*

*"According to the documents the groups in
contact with the I.R.A. included:*

*"*The Fourth International in Brussels,
which has organized pro-I.R.A. demonstrations
in several European cities.*

*"*The Maoist Army of Japan, which was
linked to the Lod Airport massacre in Israel.*

*"*The Arab Popular Front for the Liberation
of Palestine.*

*"*The Black Panthers organization in the
United States.*

"*The Turkish Liberation Front.

*"*The Underground movement in several
African countries."*

*"DUBLIN—Almost every nation has its
revolutionaries these days, men or women
espousing violent or peaceful changes in or for
their countries, and Cathal Goulding is one of
the Irish Republic's reigning avowed rebels.*

*"Chief of Staff of the official wing of the Irish
Republican Army, he seeks the ouster of the
British from Northern Ireland and its unifi-
cation with the south here in a socialist state.*

*"At the moment, he favors political action to
attain those goals, unlike the I.R.A. Provision-
als who believe they can be achieved only with
violence.*

*"But Goulding has employed violence; he
admits his officials are armed and have used
their weapons; he has threatened killings, and
he acknowledges some 'coercion' may be necessary to develop the kind of state he envisions.*

> *"Goulding has been called a Marxist, favors the dialetic approach when reviewing Ireland's problems, and intersperses his reflections on Ireland and its future with such phrases as 'national liberation . . . imperialism . . . the socialist world.'*
>
> *"He said he favors the 'nationalization' of Ireland's lead and zinc, silver and copper mines, and he would apparently confiscate such large British-owned estates as that belonging to the Duke of Devonshire. He says he wants for Ireland a political system akin to that imposed on Cuba by Fidel Castro.*
>
> *"Goulding said he is an exponent of Marxism, but not of the Soviet or Chinese stripe, and delivered these statements:*
>
> *" 'We must turn our revolutionary campaign into every activity, including politics.*
>
> *" 'We can't have socialism without national liberation and we can't have national liberation without the unity of the working class' " (Tom* Lambert, *LA Times,* March 18, 1973, p. 4).

This series of frankly-stated Marxist objectives proves that the war in Ireland is not primarily between Catholics and Protestants. Behind the turmoil are antichrists working for the real objectives of the" Unify Ireland Movement": to turn Ireland into a Red Marxist-socialist state with power to control business, so that businessmen could neither buy nor sell unless they cooperated with the socialist state. This is a sure mark of a deceptive movement which is a typical forerunner of the great Antichrist to come.

This man, Goulding, is at the top of the Irish Republican Army, which ostensibly fights for Irish unity. But in a moment of candor, he confesses his true motivation—to make Ireland socialistic. (He really means "communistic," however, for as he put it *"like Cuba."*)

CHAPTER 6

Setting The Stage

The world longs for peace, and the American government is making every concession to the communist enemy of God to get it. But peace will not come, except temporarily. Despite their peace propaganda, Communists keep subverting one country after another.

A recent issue of "The World Crisis," published by Kilbrittain Newspapers, Ltd. of Dublin, Ireland, revealed a partial timetable for planned Russian world domination.

> ". . . Russia is known to be planning a new offensive in the Middle East. Our precise and categorical information is that Russia plans to have totally taken over all Southern Africa, all the Middle East and Western Europe by January 8-9, 1984 . . . Detente is designed only to encourage us to sleep."

The Bible warns us that the hope for world peace is

illusory until the Prince of Peace returns and rids the earth of rebellion against God, the true source of all wars. For as long as man is at war with God, he will be at war with his fellow man.

The great war that is certain to come will probably be directly or indirectly connected with God-defying communism. It will be caused by the communist mania to conquer the world. Beyond this, the Antichrist will head an empire perhaps designed to insure that the Soviet Union will not again rise to power. He will be a man of war (Rev. 13:4), as well as a political genius and economic dictator.

Surely it must be evident that the closer we get to the fulfillment of a biblical prophecy, the more light will break forth upon it. As an example: In Ezekiel 38, Ethiopia and Libya are declared to someday become the allies of the Soviet-led confederacy which is to invade the Holy Land in the days of Israel's return from the diaspora. Only ten years ago the governments of both countries seemed firmly established in the Western camp. Today, both are completely dominated by the Soviet Union.

Still another example: In the first (1917) edition of the Scofield Bible, the footnote on Exekiel 38 correctly identifies the Soviet Union as the future invader of Israel. But nowhere in the Scofield notes are the reason or motivation of Russia mentioned. Yet that motivation is stated by Ezekiel in chapter 38 as, "I will. . . put hooks into thy jaws and I will bring forth (v. 4). . . thou shalt come from thy place out of the north parts (v. 15). . . like a cloud to cover the land (v. 16). . . to carry away silver and gold, to take away cattle and goods, to take a great spoil (v. 13)." The value of Middle Eastern petroleum was, of course, unknown in Ezekiel's day, and remained so until recently. Petroleum is the greatest prize in today's world.

We face the grave fact that modern civilization is wholly dependent upon energy. The greatest concentrations of petroleum energy in the world are in the Middle Eastern oil states. Standing between several of them and the Soviets, with their lust for conquest and potential recurrent famine conditions, are Jordan and Israel, the Arab oil states, the United States, and to some measure, Western Europe.

Every day's news brings this great confrontation even more into likelihood. Events are fulfilling prophetic conditions with rapidity. Confrontation between the Soviet-led nations and the Western powers in the Middle East looms as a certainty.

The War of Exekiel 38, 39

This battle has not had the wide attention among conservative scholars that it deserves. World affairs which are even now setting the stage for the battle described in Ezekiel 38 are too often ignored as having no immediate meaning in relation to biblical prophecy. This is an error which must be rectified.

Why *cannot* the battle in the thirty-ninth chapter of Ezekiel refer to Armageddon? There are at least nine major differences between them:

(1) The different locations of the battles; (2) the different opponents; (3) the different outcomes; (4) the different aftermaths; (5) the different purposes; (6) the different consequences; i.e., the shift in the balance of world power which will occur with five-sixths of the Soviet confederacy's invading army destroyed; (7) the invasion and defeat of the Soviet armies will furnish the climate for the rise of the Antichrist; (8) the climax of Armageddon, on the

other hand, spells the doom of the Antichrist; (9) the building of the Temple, which logically follows chapters 38-39 as described in Ezekiel 40-48, is nowhere declared to be the result of Christ's second coming, but very naturally could follow the defeat of the Soviet-led confederacy as depicted in Ezekiel 38-39.

After the invasion of Israel, according to the prophecy in the book of Daniel, there is to be a time lapse of about three and a half years, after which the Jews are to make a seven-year covenant with the Antichrist to allow them to rebuild their Temple. Having then done so, their covenant is to be "broken in the midst thereof," and the Antichrist is to declare himself to be the Messiah at the time of the opening of the Temple. This is explained in Daniel 7:25 and confirmed in II Thessalonians 2:3-5, where St. Paul refers to the Antichrist as appearing in the "temple of God."

All this would be difficult to harmonize if the battle of Ezekiel were in fact to be the same as Armageddon. But it simply is not possible, regardless of what other scholars have written.

Today's Superpowers

There are at present, only two superpowers, the United States and the United Soviet Socialist Republic. Africa is no power at all; India lacks military might; China is a potential, but not an actual, superpower. Europe is disunited and its constituent nations are frequently at odds with each other.

When the Soviet Union makes its desperate gamble for the energy of the Middle East, it will perhaps be impelled, as we have suggested, by lust for strategic conquest plus the desire to control one of the major energy sources of the world as a bargaining pawn for food. Exportable food supplies are now controlled eighty-five percent by the United States and Canada.

When Russia is ultimately defeated, there will be a serious shift in the balance of power. Then there will exist an emerging China and the United States.

Europe, now playing with the idea of a Common Market, will certainly then realize that she, if she unites, can become the third great world power. By such a union it will possess the technology and resources to guard against conquest by Red China or any organized combination of lesser nations, and even against economic competition with America.

This state of affairs is made to order for the brilliant statesman, the opportunist, who will emerge from one of the nations of the former Greek and Roman empires. The Bible indicates this person will be the Antichrist. Because of his success in re-establishing a united Europe like that of ancient Rome, inspired by Satan, he incites the hope of bringing peace by a new balance of world power based upon a united Europe, standing well above a defeated Russia, an emerging China and a triumphant United States.

The revival of the Greek and Roman Empires and a new Europe is a certainty by the measurements of both the prophecies of Daniel and the stern reality of the yearnings of a United Europe, determined never again to be a pawn between East and West, between the oil countries and the prosperous Americas.

Europe, as Hitler showed, can, if it is forced, be self-sufficient, powerful economically, with food and military might. Though it is sick and disunited today, Europe with its huge, total population can become the mightiest single power on earth in every sense of the word. Under the Antichrist, with the Soviet Union no longer complicating things, it will do just that.

Thus, what is sketched here is a possible scenario for things to come, logically and likely. It also fits the shape of things to come as predicted in the prophetic Word, especially as reflected in Ezekiel 38-39, which forms one of the most specific and datable prophecies in the Bible.

Ezekiel's Prophecy

For our purposes, in order to see the full meaning of the great Mideast invasion described in Ezekiel 38, we need the answers to four questions: Who are the nations mentioned? What are they to do? What is the outcome? What is the period of time actually indicated?

The last three questions are easily determined. There is to be an invasion of Israel by a confederacy of northern European, Soviet-led nations, in the time period after Israel is gathered out of the various countries of the world and restored to her historic land.

This Soviet-led confederacy is to lose five-sixths of its forces and also suffer great destruction in her homeland. All of this, as we have shown, will result in a radical shift in the balance of world power. Europe will be shaken by threats to her main energy sources and the possibility of the triumph of communism. As a consequence, she will unite, saying, "Never again!" This will be caused by the Antichrist, the ruler who seeks world power and promises security and prosperity if all power is given to him. A Europe thus united will be an ideal base for his lust for world empire.

While recently in the Middle East on a fact-finding mission, I was careful to observe the world situation as reflected in the growing crisis there. In order to understand the mounting tensions from the long-range point of view, review the thirty-eighth chapter of the book of Ezekiel. I have researched very carefully the lexicons, commentaries, Bible dictionaries and Bible encyclopedias to check every important word which appears in the thirty-eighth and thirty-ninth chapters. I have preached on these two chapters possibly ten times in the last ten years, but events in the Middle East are moving so rapidly that we must continually re-examine today's unfolding history in light of biblical prophecy.

To some readers, the message of this book is perhaps new and strange. We must remember that the book of Ezekiel was written (c. 575 B.C.) in Babylon by Ezekiel, who was both a priest and a prophet. He was also a great writer of Scripture. Ezekiel had been in Babylon for a long time as a captive. God moved across his mind as a harpist moves his fingers across the strings of a harp, to reveal the truth of what will someday happen to the nations with whom Israel is related. We must not think that Ezekiel wrote only for his day.

Ezekiel mentions great nations which, in his day, were not yet born in their modern form. But more importantly for this study we should realize that Ezekiel refers to these areas, countries and peoples by names which were familiar to him. Our task, therefore, in correctly understanding this portion of Ezekiel is to know what he meant by the names he uses. It will do little good for us to recognize them only by their current or modern names because the names by which we know them may be modern in origin, and the contemporaneous geographical and political boundaries may have changed many times during the centuries since Ezekiel wrote. The question is, "What did those names of the nations mean to Ezekiel in his day and time?"

Then, projecting to the date of the far distant future era which is very carefully identified by Ezekiel, we ask which of those nations today occupies the particular places he had in mind? What does Ezekiel tell us is going to take place among them? We read from Ezekiel 38:1 the ancient tribal names:

"The Word of the Lord came unto me saying, Son of Man set thy face." This a typical, biblical description of the prophet who is being commanded to denounce a nation or a people. In other words, Ezekiel was told to deliver a prophecy against a nation or a group of nations.

"Against God." The name the Lord gave the leading person, the dictator, the prince, as he addresses him through the prophecy.

"Of the land of Magog." Here we are on firm ground, for Magog was the grandson of Noah and his descendants settled in what is now called Russia. St. Ambrose in *De Excessu Fratris*, A.D. 378, identified Magog as the Goths. In the Talmud (L. Gensburg, 1889/58), Magog is the country of the White Huns or southern Russia. Josephus identified Magog with the Scythians (S.J. 1, 6, 25).

"The chief prince of Meshech and Tubal." So it reads in the King James Version, but the Revised Version reads, "Set thy face against Gog of the land of Magog, of *Rosh,* Meshech and Tubal." "Rosh" is a proper name that has been poorly translated in the

K.J.V. as "chief prince." It takes little imagination to realize that this particular string of names in Ezekiel 38-39 deals with nations and peoples who in Ezekiel's day were settled in what we now call the Soviet Union. This is no fantasy. You will notice this same interpretation in the footnotes of the Scofield Bible. There it says, "The reference is to the powers in the north of Europe headed by Russia." With that alone we would have enough to indicate that prominent Bible scholars believe that Russia is meant. But we will not be content with that because we also have here the root of the name of Russia, "Rosh." We realize that vowels in names may change, but often their consonants remain the same. Meshech is, of course, related to Muscovy, and that was the name of the tribe that eventually chose "Moscow" as its capital. "Tubal," also mentioned here, was the name of the tribe that eventually chose "Tobolsk" as its capital city.

Rosh

This name does not appear in the King James Version because King James' translators did not realize that "Rosh" (in Ezekiel 38:3) was a name. Instead they translated "Rosh" as "chief prince." Of the fact that "Rosh" is a proper name, William Kelly, in *Notes on Ezekiel* (pp. 192-193) says:

> *"It is true that 'Rosh', when the context requires it to be a common appellative, means 'head,' or 'chief.' But it is this sense which in the present instance brings in confusion. There can be no doubt therefore that it must be taken as a proper name, and here not as a man as in Genesis 26:2, if the common reading stands, but*

*as a race. This at once furnishes a suitable
sense, which is strengthened by the term which
precedes it as well as by those that follow . . .
Meshech and Tubal fix Rosh as meaning a
Gentile name Rosh."*

As to the identification of "Rosh," it is not hard to
see that we are here very near the language root of
Russia. But that alone is not enough. Dr. Louis
Bauman wrote:

"Our Lord's own Bible, the Septuagint, speaks of
'Gog' as 'the prince of Rosh.' If modern lexico-
graphers are consulted as to what nation now represents "Rosh," nearly all of them, together with most
expositors, say, Russia." (*Russian Events in the
Light of Bible Prophecy,* p. 24).

Robert Lowth, Bishop of London, observed:

*"Rosh, taken as a proper name in Ezekiel,
signifies the inhabitants of Scythia, from whom
the modern Russians derived their modern
name."* (Bauman, p. 24)

The identification of "Rosh" is confirmed by the
associated names which follow:

Magog. The land of Gog, the leader (literally
"mountain") is called Magog. Here again we are on
firm ground in identifying the Soviet Union in this
prophecy.

Dr. Gaebelein says:

*"Magog's land was located in what is called
today the Caucasus and the adjoining steppes . .
. the ancient Scythians." (The Prophet Ezekiel,*
p. 257)

Dr.Bauman adds:

> *"Josephus said, 'Magog founded those that from him were named Magogites, but who by the Greeks were called Scythians. The Scythians themselves have a tradition that their ancestors originally came forth from Araxes in Armenia (i.e., that part of Armenia which is in the Soviet Union now).' "*

The Japhetic race (Japheth was the father of Magog, Gen. 10:1, 2), comprised those whom the Greeks called, "Sarmatians," a mixture of Medes and Scythians who emigrated in small bands to the region of the Black Sea and extended from the Baltic to the Urals. Today their descendants are known as Tartars, Coassacks, Finns, Kalmuks and Mongols.

The *New Schaff-Herzog Encyclopedia of Religious Knowledge* says:

> *"A stricter geographical location would place Magog's dwelling between Armenia and Media, perhaps on the shores of the Araxes. But the people seem to have extended farther north across the Caucasus, filling there the extreme northern horizon of the Hebrews (Ezek. 38:15, 39:2). This is the way Meshech and Tubal are often mentioned in the Assyrian inscriptions (Mushku and Tabal: Greek Moschoi and Tibarenoi)."* (Vol. 5, p. 14)

Meshech. According to Bauman, Gesenius, the Hebrew lexicographer, also identified Meshech as Moscow or Muscovy. Russians are known as "Muscovites," a name which comes from the root, Meshech.

Tubal. Gesenius also identified Tubal as a part of Russia (Tobolsk), the earliest province of Asiatic what the rider of a horse does when he puts bits into the horse's mouth, or a fisherman when he puts a hook into the mouth of the fish. It means control by force. This force is to be the motivation which draws the confederacy south.

The prophecy continues by naming more allied nations listed with those that have already been named as the chief movers in this great invasion army. In verse 5, "Persia" and then "Cush" and "Put." These same names in the King James Version read "Ethiopia" and "Libya." In the case of the latter two names, the King James Version is correct in its interpretation.

Who is Persia in this reference? At the time Ezekiel wrote this prophecy, Cyrus the Great had not yet conquered Persia. So Ezekiel probably referred to those nations, peoples and tribes known as Aryans who inhabited what is called today Armenian Russia, the northern part of Iraq, and also the northern part of what today is called Iran. We cannot, therefore, definitely say that this prophecy refers to Persia or Iran as we know it today. It may; it may not. We do not know.

Gomer. Ezekiel 38:6 reads, "Gomer, and all his hordes." The King James Version says "bands," but it means traveling bands of men or soldiers. Gomer was another immediate descendant of Noah and his descendants who settled to the north of the Black Sea in what is today called the Soviet Union. The inhabitants of that area then moved westward into what is today known as Germany. The implication, I think, is very clear that at least Easy Germany is included within the scope of this prophecy.

This reference is to eastern Germany and Poland. Gibbon (*Decline and Fall of the Roman Empire*) says the German detachment of Gomer marched under the banner of Ashkenaz, the son of Gomer (vol. 1, p. 204). Gibbon was referring to the conquest of what is now Poland, part of Russia and East Germany in the generations following Noah's flood. Ashkenaz was the great grandson of Noah.

Jews from Germany, Russia and Poland are referred to, even now, as "Ashkenazim." Proof of this is plentiful:

(1) *The Encyclopaedia Britannica* (vol. 10, p. 511) says Gomer represents the people known as the Cimmerians and originated in the district north of the Black Sea, i.e., Russia. Of course, they spread westward into Germany by the time of Ezekiel. We must think of their location at Ezekiel's time, not later, as read his prediction, but it certainly means East Germany today.

(2) Herodotus, the famed "father of history," said in his account of Scythia that the Cimmerians inhabited South Russia. From there they moved north toward Germany as the centuries passed.

(3) Josephus, the great first-century historian, called the sons of Ashkenaz "the Rheginians" and a map of the ancient Roman Empire places them in the area of Czechoslovakia and Germany.

(4) The Talmud, the Jewish commentary of ancient times, flatly states that the sons of Gomer are Germans, in the sense that the tribes of Gomer and his descendants eventually followed the Danube River from Russia into Germany.

Togarmah. Ezekiel also mentions another nation, "the house of Togarmah of the north quarters." Ezekiel was writing in Babylon and the next country north is what we call Asia Minor, divided today among Turkey, Iran, Iraq and the Soviet Union.

St. Peter's Basilica in Rome, Italy

During the reign of the Antichrist, this city will be the capital of the one-world religion, an alliance of apostate Catholicism and Protestantism, directed by the False Prophet. This scriptural leader will deceive many and cause all to worship the "Image of the Beast."

The Isle of Patmos
Dr. W.S. McBirnie, Chaplain Ray and Carl Newton visit the island where the Apostle John first envisioned the rise and rule of the Antichrist centuries ago. While held captive on Patmos, John wrote The Revelation.

The Roman Empire
Shown here at the time of Augustus Caesar's death, enlarged
during the first century, the Roman Empire approximates the
territories of The European Common Market. Bible scholars
believe the Antichrist will emerge from one of the Market's
member nations.

The Golden Gate, Jerusalem
Located in the ancient Eastern Wall,
biblical scholars believe this gate is
the site where Christ will enter
Jerusalem at His Second Coming.

Roman Senate House
The center of the Roman world, seen
here as it has been restored to duplicate
its appearance in the first century
before Christ. Near here, St. Peter and
St. Paul were imprisoned.

Ancient Roman Street

Author W.S. McBirnie stands on a Roman street, built in the days of the Caesars. Many such roads, surfaced by heavy stones, have endured until modern times and are still usable.

Caesar Augustus

Augustus, the Roman Emperor who ordered a world-wide tax shortly before the birth of Christ, first ruled the united Roman Empire. Although after his death the Empire was enlarged to include Britain, Augustus ruled the area many believe will produce the Antichrist.

The Roman Forum and Coliseum
This famous structure, a marvel of the ancient world, was the site of countless murders of first- and second-century believers.

Incense Altar Upon this rock altar, ancient Romans burned incense to the image of Caesar. Caesar worship was the first example of the spirit of the Antichrist.

The Basilica of St. John Lateran in Rome. Here the heads of St. Peter and St. Paul now rest above the high altar. The basilica was erected, however, in memory of St. John, who told us of the Antichrist.

Exterior, The Basilica of St. John Lateran

The Church of the Nativity, Bethlehem, Israel Jesus was born in Bethlehem and lived in obscurity for 30 years. The Antichrist will doubtlessly follow this pattern. He may be active on earth today as a young political leader not yet revealed in all his dreadful ability to become Satan's christ.

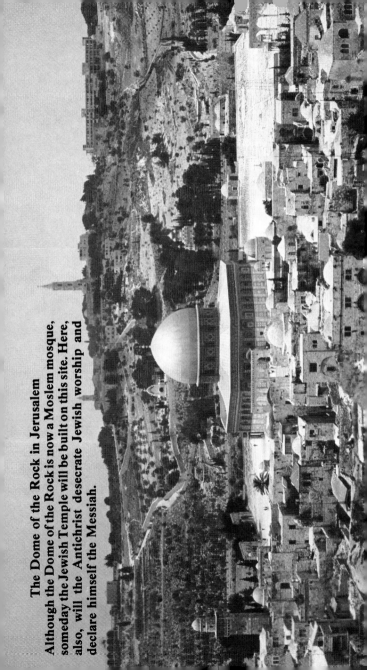

The Dome of the Rock in Jerusalem
Although the Dome of the Rock is now a Moslem mosque, someday the Jewish Temple will be built on this site. Here, also, will the Antichrist desecrate Jewish worship and declare himself the Messiah.

Babylon's Ishtar Gates

St. Peter is credited with founding the church at Babylon, which in turn helped evangelize Iraq and Iran. Since the city was no longer a world power in the first century, the name became symbolic of the then-present power, Rome.

Antioch, Turkey
This gigantic head is of Antiochus, who history says was the king to first pollute the Temple in Jerusalem. Antiochus sacrificed a pig on the holy altar, thus desecrating the Temple. Both the prophet Daniel and Jesus talked of this "Abomination of Desolation," and warned that another similar desecration would occur during the reign of the coming Antichrist.

Ephesus

Pictured are the ruins of the main church pastored by St. John. This congregation was the first to read John's account of the Antichrist.

The Cave of St. John Located on the Isle of Patmos, Greece, this may have been the site of John's supernatural vision and his writing of The Revelation.

Ezekiel most specifically refers to these people as "of the north quarters," thus including yet another portion of the Soviet Union in terms of the geographical occupation of the tribe of Togarmah in that day.

Togarmah was the second son of Gomer, and his descendants occupied northern and eastern Turkey, and Turkestan, which is now part of the Soviet Union. The prophecy of Ezekiel speaks of "Togarmah and all his bands (tribes)," so we are safe in looking toward the southern part of the Soviet Union which in other days was composed of many small nations such as Armenia and including some of the Tartar hordes who lived in Asia south of the Sea of Aral and between that sea and the Caspian Sea.

Dr. Raymond Edman, the late president of Wheaton College, affirmed:

> *"The ancestors of modern Armenia claim that the father of their race, Haik, was the son of Togarmah." (Sunday School Times,* quoted by Bauman).

Dr. Harry Rimmer wrote:

> *"Togarmah has always been the land we call Armenia (i.e., a part of the Soviet Union)." (The Coming War and the Rise of Russia,* p. 62)

So all these countries described by Ezekiel by the names with which he was familier in 570 B.C., are to be linked in a terrible invasion army. The scope of it ranges from Africa to Asiatic Siberia; from Germany to the Balkans; from Moscow to many Arab nations in the Middle East and Africa, along the southern coast of the Mediterranean. Think of it. All these bloody, communist nations, uninhibited by Christian tradition, converging on the land of Israel and her neighbors! Gog, the leader, comes from the north, but his allies come from every direction of the compass. The invasion group consists of the Huns, the Mongol hordes, the Cossacks, some Arabs, the Africans and the Russians, all moving toward the land-bridge of three continents, toward the land of Israel, and that of her immediate neighbors! Though this war is geographically focused, it is a world war. Perhaps it will even be called "World War III."

CHAPTER 7

The Opponents

Ezekiel 38:13, 18 lists the nations who will oppose the great Northern Confederacy. He used the Ancient names of these nations, as we have said. Who are they?

Israel. This is the Israel gathered out of the dispersion, filled with those who have re-established their ancient country, "who dwell safely in unwalled villages." There is no mistaking the main objective of the Soviet confederacy: It is Israel. However, we would be greatly mistaken to identify this by the boundaries of modern Israel. Part of ancient Israel is located in Jordan, which tells us the great battle will be fought in the "valley of the passengers on the east of the sea." The "sea" is Galilee, and the "valley of the passengers" is probably the valley lying to east of the sea, well within modern Jordanian territory. It also continues east of the Dead Sea southwards. Interestingly, Dr. Taylor, in his paraphrase of this passage translates the location as the Dead Sea.

Sheba. The queen of Sheba who visited King

Russia to be colonized. Moscow was a district as well as a city. So, apparently, was Tobolsk. Moscow or Moscovy is of Europe; Tobolsk is of Asia. The Soviet Union encompasses them both. Hence Magog is the designated name in the Bible of the united Asiatic and European Soviet Union, consisting of Rosh, Mescheck and Tubal. Speaking of the migration of some Asiatics who were originally of Tubal, Rev W.M.H. Milner, in *The Russian Chapters of Ezekiel,* says:

> *"The historian Gibbon, in the forty-second chapter of his "Decline and Fall of the Roman Empire," referring to the middle of the sixth century A.D., deals with the question thus:*

> *" 'The wild people who dwelt or wandered in the plains of Russia, Lithuania and Poland might be reduced, in the age of Justinian, under the two great families of the Bulgarians and the Sclavonians. According to the Greek writers the former, who touched the Euxine and the lake Maeotic, derived from the Huns their name or descent; and it is needless to renew the simple and well-known picture of Tartar manners. They were bold and dextrous archers, who drank the milk and feasted on the flesh of their horses.' "*

Then says God to Ezekiel, "Prophesy against him (the prince who heads this confederation), and say, Thus saith the Lord God; Behold, I am against thee, O Gog, the prince of Rosh, Meshech and Tubal: And I will turn thee back and put hooks into thy jaws." Here is another familiar biblical phrase. It describes

Solomon probably came from the south of Arabia, perhaps in the area of the oil-rich countries of the southwestern edge of the Arabian peninsula (see the Schaff-Hertsog encyclopedia, p. 249). Archaeologists have confirmed this, notably W.F. Albright and Wendell Phillips in their expedition there in 1947.

Dedan. Davis' *Dictionary of the Bible* identifies this nation as the Arabs of the northern part of the Arabian desert, notably in Saudi Arabia today. It is also very instructive that Saudi Arabia has refused to accept Arab socialism, but instead has remained loyal to the free world. Startlingly, the ancient trading city is identifiable as Dedan on biblical maps today as being well within Saudi Arabia.

Jordan. Though the bitterness between modern Israel and Jordan remains acute, it is notably less violent than the hatred between Syria and Israel. Pressure from the Arab world is upon the Hashemite Kingdom to resist any settlement with Israel which would legitimatize Israel as a nation. However, the recent history-making visit of President Sadat of Egypt to Israel may mark the beginning of an alliance against Russia which must come someday if not soon.

This writer, who has journeyed thirty-seven times through most of the Middle East, offers an opinion that Jordan and Israel are, dispite their quarrels, natural allies, and if it were not for the pressure upon Jordan from the rest of the Arab world, peace could be resolved to the complete satisfaction of both nations. Jordan and Israel, as sacred lands, are both dear to the hearts of almost all people in the United States, and these two nations would be instantly defended by the United States in case either of them were threatened seriously by others. At least, such is the present reality. Further, it would behoove both Israel and Jordan to look well into Ezekiel's prophecy, since the common threat of communism will someday unite them to some degree, whether or not they can believe this at the moment. War makes strange bedfellows, and as surely as the Bible is true, these two nations will some day unite their intentions to oppose the Russian horde.

Interestingly, one of the prophecies concerning the Northern Confederacy mentions the area now known as Jordan by name. There is an entire passage in Daniel given to the same events as those Ezekiel saw. In this passage, Gog is called the "king of the North." and is predicted to enter (invade) "the glorious land (the Holy Land)."

> *"He shall enter also into the glorious land, and many countries shall be overthrown: but these escape out of His hand, even Edom, and Moab, and the chief of the children of Ammon"* *(Dan. 11:41).*

The present boundaries of Jordan encompass the countries of Edom, Moab and the land of Ammon. Today Jordan has Amman (ancient Rabath-Ammon) as her capital city. Ezekiel's vision notes the Arabian nations, including Dedan and Sheba (Dedan is another ancient name for Saudi Arabia), are to challenge the Soviet confederacy. Daniel is even more specific. He says Jordan will escape. Daniel notes also that Ethiopia and Libya will be allied with Russia. The two prophecies of Daniel and Ezekiel fit each other with beautiful precision!

Now, we return to Ezekiel's prophecy for the identity of the last challengers of the Soviet invaders.

The Merchants of Tarshish

Of all the groups and nations mentioned in Ezekiel, this is the hardest to identify. Attempts have been made to identify "Tarshish" with "Tarsus" in Turkey. If this were so, the whole prophecy would be confused and meaningless. Certainly there is no significance to Turkey as a world power today. Were Turkey the only ally of Israel, Sheba and Dedan, since these few Jewish and Arab peoples are not strong themselves (though they do have the advantage of being on the ground which is to be invaded), there would be little resistance indeed to the Soviet advance. In any case, Tarsus was never mentioned in ancient literature as standing for Turkey as a whole.

Davis, in his *Dictionary of the Bible* (p. 723) says this of Tarshish:

> *"It was a distant land (Isa. 66:19). . . It is believed that Tarshish was Tartessus, in the south of Spain, near Gibraltar (Herod LV. 152). . . Ships of Tarshish were originally ships trading to and from Tarshish, but ultimately ships of first-rate magnitude to whatever place their voyages may have been made."*

Only in the past half-dozen years has much light been thrown on the historic location of ancient Tarshish. Books and articles in learned archaeological journals written before that time now seem to have rather limited value. In some instances, they are more confusing than helpful, dispite the prestige of their authors. The reasons for certainty of identification are found in recent archaeological discoveries which confirm that ancient authorities were right all along in their identification of Tarshish as a Western European colonizing power based in Spain.

The justly-famous archaeologist, William F. Albright, for example, was convinced that Tarshish was located on the island of Sardinia, despite clear indications, even from ancient Roman writers, that Tarshish was founded shortly after the Trojan War (1109 B.C.) near the present city of Cadiz in western Spain. Commenting on such ideas that the Phoenicians were limited in their westward outreach, the noted Phoenician scholar, Sabatino Moscoti, says:

> *"In recent times flaws have been found in this attitude. Even archaeologists are beginning to place Phoenician expansion in the Mediterranean at an earlier period. They claim that lack of evidence is no argument and refer to the information contained in archaeological findings and in inscriptions which so far have been neglected.*
>
> *"Furthermore, at the time of Solomon, the Bible mentions the merchant fleet of Tyre, capable of undertaking long and difficult crossings. It mentions specifically a 'navy of Tarshish,' and in all likelihood, Tarshish must be identified with the southwestern area of Spain.*
>
> *"Now it is quite possible that in this case the expression may mean 'ocean-going navy,' but nevertheless the reference exists and so, since we have no reason to doubt the veracity of biblical sources in this respect, it seems probable that Phoenician navigators had penetrated to the far west as early as the tenth century and obviously had to make use of numerous landing-stages.*
>
> *". . . it must be kept in mind that the Phoenicians did not only settle in places where colonies subsequently developed, but also founded trading posts in regions ethnically and*

politically different, and either remained there as small settlements or dissolved.

"Proceeding farther along the African coast of the Mediterranean, the earliest colony, traditionally, is Utica. Velleius Paterculus says that the Phoenician fleet which controlled the seas founded Cadiz about eighty years after the fall of Troy and Utica a little later. Since he ascribes the fall of Troy elsewhere to c. 1190 B.C., Cadiz appears to have been founded c.1110 and Utica c. 1100." (The World of the Phoenicians, pp. 95, 96, 97, 98, 99).

Tarshish

Perhaps we have enough information now to clear up much of the mystery of what and where Tarshish was. Moscoti has set out the opinion that Tarshish at first was a reference to Tarsus in Asia Minor, and the same name was later given to Tartessus in Spain because of the similarity of the consonants in the name itself.

Perhaps this may have originally been the case. But from about 1010 B.C., it is clear that the Phoenicians were in western Spain beyond Gibraltar at the place the Romans called Gades, today known as Cadiz. The colonial trading post of Tarshish (which came to be its name) was located not far away at the mouth of the Guadalquivir River in southwestern Spain. Moscoti seems certain about this and observes:

"Finally, the most controversial point about Phoenician colonization concerns Spain. The colony of Cadiz goes back traditionally to the end of the twelfth century. The material from it is far later (fifth century) and the earlier remains

of other localities, which can probably be ascribed to the eighth century, are still far from the traditional date. Tarshish (Tartessus) was probably to the north of Cadiz, at the source of the Guadalquivir. The most likely opinions place it on the site of Asta Regia. The identification of Tarshish with Tartessus leads us to believe that we can ascribe Phoenician settlement in Spain to the tenth century, if not to the traditional date. Another reason for earlier ascriptions of the archaeological data is provided by Mazar's mission in Spain in 1957, the result of which have not yet been published. Mazar asserts that there are archaelogical traces of the Phoenicians in Spain going back at least as far as the ninth century." (Moscoti, p. 100)

The German writer, Gerhard Herm, traces Tarshish in much the same way:

"The routes which the Carthaginian ships followed were essentially the same as those which the East Phoenicians had chosen. Above all, they linked Tartessus, the land rich in minerals, to the colonized countries of the east, including Greece. But where was Tartessus?

"One can only say with certainty that this mysterious place was an area in southern Spain. Strabo thought it was a river 'with springs rich in silver,' whereas Herodotus told of a king who ruled over Tartessus, and so must have thought it was a country. If one pieces together everything which the classical authors wrote about it, one gets the picture of a large community which took its name from a river, the

*present-day Guadalquivir, and which lay on an
island between the two arms of its estuary. It was
rich, because the river came from the 'silver
mountains' and brought great quantities of the
different noble and nonferrous metals with it.
Especially tin, copper, gold and silver.*

*"If this description is approximately accu-
rate, the Iberian El Dorado must have been
situated near the sherry town of Jerez de la
Frontera, between the Guadalquivir and the Rio
Guadalete, because the first of these two rivers
does not have two mouths. The silver mountains, however, were identical with the Sierra
Morena, a mountain range in which there are in
fact rich deposits of copper and also smaller
quantities of silver and gold. But there is, at any
rate now, no tin there."* (Herm, p. 204)

It is evident that the city of Tarshish, as such,
ceased to exist sometime around the end of Ezekiel's
lifetime. Nevertheless, as Herm explains, the "merchants of Tarshish" continued to trade and flourish
from their better port of Cadiz.

*"In 500 B.C. Tartessus disappeared from
sight so mysteriously that Plato was inspired—
or so one imagines—to base his Atlantis myth
on it. The facts which remain are: From their old
base of Cadiz (which lies opposite the mouth of
the Rio Guadelete), the Carthaginians traded
with an Iberian people, who must already have
had skilled miners, and then transported the ore
back to the Mediterranean. In addition, they
appear to have also bought or occupied land
there, because an old chronicle, based on Greek
texts, the De ora maratima of the Latin poet*

> *Avienus, speaks of many 'peoples and towns,'*
> *beyond the Pillars of Hercules, which were ruled*
> *by the Carthaginians. Modern historians have*
> *even suggested that more than twenty ports of*
> *varying sizes on the Atlantic coast of Spain and*
> *Portugal owe their origins to West Phoenician*
> *activities and that the North African town ruled*
> *almost half of Spain. The limits of the Cartha-*
> *ginian sphere of influence are generally indi-*
> *cated today by a line from the mouth of the Ebro*
> *to that of the Tagus. Hannibal later advanced as*
> *far as Helmantike, present-day Salamanca.*
> *Carthgena (New Carthage), Saguntum and*
> *possibly Malaga were built by his countrymen."*

• Herm raises the intriquing possibility that some Jews may have sailed on the ships of Tarshish.

> *"Among other things, these and later settle-*
> *ments in Iberia gave rise to a strange rumor,*
> *which claims that the many Spanish Jews who,*
> *until their banishment in the late fifteenth cen-*
> *tury had played such an important and splendid*
> *role in the commercial and spiritual life of the*
> *Christian territory between Gibraltar and the*
> *Pyrenees, were in fact genuine descendants of*
> *the Phoenicians, whom they so much resembled.*
> *To support the thesis, it is claimed that their*
> *great number—around the year 1490 there were*
> *in Spain more than 300,000 Jews—cannot even*
> *be explained by assuming that large numbers of*
> *them immigrated together with the Moors. And*
> *further, so say the supporters of this theory, after*
> *the Reconquista, no one could really tell the*
> *difference between Semitic-looking people of*
> *Jewish, Islamic or Christian belief. Whoever*

*looked like a Jew or a 'Marrano (literally: pig),'
a baptized Jew, was considered to be one. And
since the Phoenicians or their descendants were
not very different from genuine Jews or their
descendants, the suspicion gains in probability
that there were perhaps many, many great-
grandnephews of Carthaginian merchants
among the Sephardim who were banished by the
Grand Inquisitor Troquemada to North Africa,
Turkey or to South America and who there
established their impressive money dynasties."*
(Herm, p. 205-206)

Tartessus

The most famous trading or merchant nation in the
Middle East in the thousand years before Christ was
that of the Phoenicians. Because Tartessus became
their famed outpost, the name, as we have seen, was
somehow changed to Tarshish. The entire Eastern
trading fleet, it has been determined, was referred to
as "the ships of Tarshish," and the Phoenicians who
traveled through the Mediterranean beyond Gibraltar were called "the merchants of Tarshish." Moscoti writes:

*"We now come to one of the main problems of
Phoenician colonial expansion: the problem of
Tarshish-Tartessus, from which an entire as-
pect of the movement of Mediterranean expansion depends. Starting with biblical source,
we read with reference to Solomon that 'the king
had at sea a navy of Tarshish with the navy of
Hiram: once in three years came the navy of
Tarshish, bringing gold and silver, ivory, apes
and peacocks.' Jeremiah mentions Tarshish*

and gold from Ophir. Ezekiel tells Tyre: 'Tarshish was thy merchant by reason of the multitude of all kind of riches; with silver, iron, tin and lead, they traded in thy fairs.' From these quotations and others of less importance, it seems clear that, even if 'navy of Tarshish' can generically mean ocean-going navy, the expression originates from the fact that Tarshish designates a city or a region in the West, particularly rich in metals. The epoch to which the texts refer can be placed around the tenth century and after it.

"Passing on to the classifical sources, it is obvious that Tartessus is a locality in southern Spain. The poet Stesichorus, who wrote c. 600 B.C. in Sicily, has left us a line quoted by Strabo which mentions 'the unlimited, silver-rooted springs of the river Tartessus.' If this refers to the river, the city is mentioned by the poet Anacreon (c. 530), again quoted by Strabo, with reference to Arganthonius, long-lived king of Tartessus. In the fifth century, but referring to an earlier period, Herodotus tells of the voyage of Kolaios to Tartessus, and of the friendship between the Phoenicians and the local king Arganthonius."

Finally, from various authors of the sixth century, the following description of Tartessus was reconstructed:

"Tartessus is an illustrious city of Iberia which takes its name from the river Baetis (Guadalquivir), formerly also called Tartessus. This river comes from the Celtic region and has its source in the 'silver mountain'; in its stream it carries, besides silver and tin, a great abun-

*dance of gold and bronze. The river Tartessus
divides into two arms when it reaches the mouth.
Tartessus, the city, stands between the two arms,
as on an island."*

"Now, is the biblical Tarshish definitely the
same as the Greek Tartessus? Recent studies
tend to give Tarshish a common rather than a
proper value, meaning 'mine' (from the Semetic
root rss). If this hypothesis is not very probable,
we must also mention the fact that Tarshish
appears in the genealogy of Genesis, together
with Elisha and Kittim, both names indicating
the iland of Cyprus, which would validate the
ancient theory, sustained by Josephus and
Eusebius, that Tarshish is to be identified with
Tarsus in Cilicia. Whatever the value of these
observations, however, it seems certain that at a
given moment Tarshish really was taken to
denote Tartessus, evidently because of the pho-
netic affinity.

"Tartessus, therefore, was a city and state
which extended far and was rich from the trade
of metals. What was its relationship with
Cadiz? It seems likely that the Phoenicians of
Cadiz succeeded to the Tartessian routes and
trade, or in any case used and supported them.
And this is why the Phoenicians founded Cadiz
in the neighborhood of the Tartessus. But where
exactly was Tartessus? The traditional Spanish
theory places the town on the site of Messa de
Asta, ancient Asta Regia, near Jerez. Others
have sought it at Donnana, at the mouth of the
Guadalquivir, but excavations have not confirmed this theory. A further possible hypothesis
places it in Huelva or in the neighborhood, on

> *the island of Saltes. In any case, the ancient city,*
> *the remains of which have not definitely been*
> *identified by archaeology, was in the region of*
> *the lower Guadalquivir." (*Moscoti, p. 231-232)

There was a good reason for the location of
Tarshish. It was the Atlantic coast point of trans-
shipment for all goods sent from the places where the
Phoenicians picked them up. For a typical example,
if they received trading items from Egypt or Israel,
they would carry them to Tarshish. There they would
be sent via another ship to, say, Britain, where they
would load British minerals, such as tin, lead, or
silver in exchange.

These ships in turn would be sent back to Tarshish
and off-loaded. Another vessel would then take these
valuable minerals on to Egypt or Israel, or perhaps
even to some other Mediterranean port. Since Tarshish was, until the mercantile operation was later
moved to the safer and more commodious port of
Cadiz, the chief early trading settlement bearing the
name "Tarshish," the name stayed. The actual
original trading post itself probably was abandoned.
No trace of it has so far been found, though the
presence of the same Phoenician traders in Cadiz
from the time of King David (1000 B.C.) is well
established in and around Cadiz in Spain and from
that time until the present. To all that has been said,
we can add the testimony of Wiseman:

> *"Traditionally, the earliest settlement in the*
> *west at Gades (Cadiz) on the Atlantic coast of*
> *Southern Spain, founded in the twelfth century*
> *on what was then a small islet at the mouth of*
> *the Guadalete, an excellent spot from which to*
> *ship the ores mined at Spanish Tarshish or*

Tartessus, some miles inland." (Wiseman, p. 280)

Moscoti tells of the purposes of the "merchants of Tarshish."

> *"The Phoenicians colonized Spain in order to obtain control of the sources of the metal trade (gold, tin, and above all, silver), which they later sold in the East at a large profit. The ancient authors tell us of this, and Diodorus, insisting on the essential value of this traffic, leads us to believe that it was the reason for, rather than the result of, the foundation of the colonies.*
>
> *"And the result was that the Phoenecians, as in the course of many years they prospered greatly thanks to commerce of this kind, sent forth many colonies, some to Sicily and its neighboring islands, and others to Libya, Sardinia and Iberia.*
>
> *"We have a series of accounts concerning the period of the colonization of Cadiz. Strabo, quoting Posidonius, tells that various expeditions were sent by the Tyrians to the Pillars of Hercules, and that the third of these expeditions resulted in the foundation of Cadiz with the sanctuary on the eastern part of the island and the city on the western part. Valleius Paterculus specifies that eighty years after the fall of Troy, c. 1110, the Tyrian fleet, which ruled the sea, founded Cadiz at the tip of Spain on an island surrounded by the ocean and separated from the mainland by a short strait; soon after, adds, the same Tyrians founded Utica. Since the sources of Utica provide the date of 1101, nothing seems to contradict the founding of Cadiz in 1110.*

> *"Cadiz was in a very important position, from the commercial point of view, since it guarded the area of the silvermines of Tartessus. It was, therefore, evidently one of the first Phoenician settlements, and the tradition according to which Lixus, on the Moroccan coast, was founded before Cadiz (as Pliny says) is also significant. From these cities, the Phoenicians could control the Mediterranean trade routes and at the same time open the routes on the Atlantic coasts (of Europe)."* (Moscoti, pp. 230, 231)

Herm agrees that the trading colonies of Tarshish included ports in Great Britain.

> *"The suffetes seem therefore to have known very well what their monopoly on the British tin trade was worth, and this in turn would indicate that such a trade did exist. It is known that the coveted metal from Britain had already reached the Continent in the Bronze Age and that the Tartessians played a part in obtaining it."* (Herm, p. 206)

Cadiz

By the time Ezekiel wrote, the "merchants (i.e., traders by sea) of Tarshish" generally operated out of Cadiz and established trading posts which had grown into sizeable colonies, up the entire coasts of Western Europe to and including Britain.

> *"At first there was no need for colonies to be numerous, since it was only possible to control navigation in certain points. This assumption of the Atlantic strongholds was obvious to the*

*ancient historians: Strabo claims that after the
Trojan War the Phoenicians sailed beyond the
Pillars of Hercules and founded cities there."*
(Moscoti, p. 231a)

Historians are indebted to the very intimate
knowledge Ezekiel had of the exact nature of the
Tarshish merchant marine and its typical items of
trade. Most of the histories of the Phoenicians gladly
quote the detailed description Ezekiel gives, which
indicates a very thorough knowledge on his part
before he became a captive in Babylon. Doubtless
Ezekiel had visited Tyre and Sidon and had seen the
Tarshish ships for himself.

So Ezekiel later wrote this description:

*"O Tyre, thou hast said, I am of perfect
beauty. Thy borders are in the midst of the seas,
thy builders have perfected thy beauty. They
have made all thy ship boards of fir trees of
Senir: they have taken cedars from Lebanon to
make masts for thee. Of the oaks of Bashan have
they made thine oars; the company of Ashurites
have made thy benches of ivory, brought of the
isles of Chittim. Fine linen with broidered work
from Egypt was that which thou spreadest forth
to be thy sail; blue and purple form the isles of
Elishah was that which covered thee. The inhabitants of Sidon and Aradus were thy
mariners: thy wise men. O Tyre, that were in
thee, were thy pilots. The ancients of Gegal and
the wise men thereof were in thee thy calkers: all
the ships of the sea with their mariners were in
thee to occupy thy merchandise.*

*"They of Persia and of Lud and of Phut were
in thine army, thy men of war: they hanged the*

shield and helmet in thee; they set forth thy
comeliness. The men of Aradus with thine army
were upon thy walls round about, and the
Gammadims were in thy towers; they hanged
their shields upon thy walls round about; they
have made thy beauty perfect. Tarshish was thy
merchant by reason of the multitude of all kind
of riches; with silver, iron, tin, and lead they
traded in thy fairs. Javan, Tubal, and Meshech,
were thy merchants: they traded the persons of
men and vessels of brass in thy market. They of
the house of Togarmah traded in thy fairs with
horses and horsemen and mules. The men of
Dedan were thy merchants; many isles were the
merchandise of thine land: they brought thee for
a present horns of ivory and ebony. Syria was
thy merchant by reason of the multitude of the
wares of thy making: they occupied in thy fairs
with emeralds, purple, and broidered work, and
fine linen, and coral, and agate. Judah, and the
land of Israel, they were thy merchants: they
traded in thy market wheat of Minnith, and
Pannag, and honey, and oil, and balm. Damas-
cus was thy merchant in the multitude of the
wares of thy making, for the multitude of all
riches; in the wine of Helbon, and white wool,
Dan also and Javan going to and fro occupied in
thy fairs: bright iron, cassia, and calamus were
in thy market. Dedan was thy merchant in
precious clothes for chariots. "Arabia, and all
the princes of Kedar, they occupied with thee, in
lambs, in rams, and goats: in these were they thy
merchants. The merchants of Sheba and
Raamah, they were thy merchants: they occupied in thy fairs with chief of all spices and with

*all previous stones and gold. Haran, and
Canneh and Eden the merchants of Sheba,
Asshur, and Chilmad were thy merchants.
These were thy merchants in all sorts of things,
in blue clothes, and broidered work, and in
chests of rich apparel, bound with cords, and
made of cedar, among thy merchandise. The
ships of Tarshish did sing of thee in thy market:
and thou wast replenished, and made very
glorious in the midst of the seas"* (Ezek. 27:3-
25).

Moscoti explains the historical value of Ezekiel's
knowledge of the Phoenician traders and locates
some of the places of trade by the merchants of
Tarshish who, of course, had originally come from
Tyre.

> *"In the first part of the passage, the allegori-
> cal image of Tyre as a great ship suggests the
> goods she traded by mentioning the materials
> used to build the ship, and the people taken as
> sailors. The wood implies Mount Hermon (of
> which Senir is peak), the Leban, Bashan
> (northeast of Lake Tiberias and) Cyprus (Chit-
> tim, from the name of the Phoenician colony
> Kition)."* (Moscoti, pp. 84-85)

Ezekiel's Meaning

We must not assume that prophets always
understood visions given to them. Daniel certainly
did not (see chapter 12). Ezekiel foresaw, but
perhaps did not fully understand the distant time
when all Israel (not merely Judah which was then in
captivity in Babylon) would be gathered out of the

nations of the whole world, and restored to their own land. It is not our purpose here to identify just who came to constitute "Israel" in captivity. Certainly Judah eventually became the main rallying force for all Israel in exile.

But a fully representative return of Israel from many nations never happened—not even in the return of the 25,000 Judeans from Babylon under Ezra—that is, until the twentieth century. So we cannot attribute the prophecy about this in the thirty-eighth chapter to a slightly later time and authorship than that of Ezekiel, by suggesting that some other writer actually experienced the events and then claimed his (forged) prophecy was made by Ezekiel himself.

Plainly, Ezekiel himself saw the return of Israel from the many nations where the people of Israel were scattered. Isaiah says they will return in "ships of Tarshish" (Isa. 60:9). Who did Ezekiel and Isaiah mean by this description which has been so long and so unnecessarily considered enigmatic? Surely the "ships of Tarshish," as envisioned by Isaiah must be identifiable in the days of the return. Who are they?

There is no reason to doubt that both prophets saw, or meant, the nations which were colonized by the Phoenicians of Tarshish. It was the Phoenician merchants who traded with and established colonies in those nations, according to abundant and lengthy quotations from scholars who specialize in Phoenician history. The only sea-link (from 1000 B.C. to 100 B.C.) between Britain and France, or Spain, or Rome for that matter, came from the actual ships of Tarshish based at first in Tarshish and later in Cadiz. So when Ezekiel mentions the merchants of Tarshish, he is referring to lands first colonized by the Phoenicians, later to be called by other names. If further proof that Ezekiel meant the Phoenician colonies, hear again from Moscoti:

> *"Beyond the Pillars of Hercules, on the Atlantic coast, new centers undoubtedly radiated from ancient Cadiz. The Ora Maritima of Avienus, in a translation from a Greek text datable soon after 500, says that the Carthaginians 'had peoples and cities' beyond the Pillars of Hercules, and the Periplus of Pseudo-Skylaz in the fourth century mentions many Carthaginian trading posts in the region. . .*
>
> *"That Carthaginian penetration was not restricted to the coastal settlements, but spread a certain distance inland in the southern region, and that it was accompanied by ethnic infiltrations is proved by the repeated reference to 'Liby-phoenicians' in the classifical sources as the population of the area in question. They were evidently Carthaginian settlers in whom the North African element played a strong part; but the term only applies to this particular zone and does not extend to Cadiz and the Atlantic coast on one side nor to Ibiza on the other."* (Moscoti, p. 234)

It was said that so busy were the Tarshish mercantile ships in 500 B.C. that in Cadiz a person need wait only an average of three days and he could get passage on a ship going to just about any port in the Mediterranean or Western Europe.

> *"There was so much maritime traffic that within three days a traveler could find a ship to take him any place he fancied in the Mediterranean."* (Herm, p. 236)

The Young Lions

This phrase carries Ezekiel's identification of the nations which shall protest or challenge the Russian-led confederacy as it invades Israel, to a further, more logical, more certain identification. "Young lions" is, in the Hebrew, "whelps" or "cubs"; obviously offspring or colonies. The "Merchants of Tarshish" were definitely colonizers. This is the plain and logical meaning of the phrase Ezekiel used.

After all, what else could he say if the mysterious vision was for a future time? He must perforce have used the terms and names of his own day. He probably did not understand the full implication of what he wrote. But he surely would say that, long after his time, a new confederacy of power would arise from the Western Atlantic nations, whose armies, riches and power might also provide the means of a future role in the preservation of Israel.

Why should we assume the ancient writers, such as Ezekiel, knew little about European areas which we know sprung into full historical life quite early? In 70 B.C. Caesar conquered Gaul which, he recorded, had already founded great cities. Several early Caesars came from Spain, notably Hadrian. How did Spain produce such men in the first century if the land of Spain were not fully civilized long before their time?

Our own concepts of the ancient world are themselves almost provincial and mythological. If Solomon could trade with Britain via the "Merchants of Tarshish" (in 950 B.C.), we must not suppose that the location and activities of Tarshish were unknown to Ezekiel in 550 B.C. Because ships in the Middle

Ages were small and distant ports unreachable, we must not conclude the same conditions prevailed in the thousand years before Christ.

In matter of fact, before the time of Jesus, there existed seagoing vessels of vastly larger size and better sea-worthiness than those Columbus used in his voyages supposedly to India, which instead accidentally resulted in the "discovery" of America. Herm deals with this:

> *"We know less about the Carthaginian merchant ships than about these warships, but they must have also been fairly large. At all events, they were larger than the boats in which the English settlers went to America in the seventeenth century. The Mayflower had a displacement of 180 tons, whereas Roman corn freighters in the third century B.C. carried well over a thousand tons, and the Carthaginian ships cannot have been much smaller."* (Herm, p. 202)

Wiseman also furnishes proof of the size and capacity of the Tarshish ships:

> *"There is reference to Phoenician maritime enterprise on the Palermo Stone inscription (c. 2200 B.C.) of forty timber-carrying ships from Byblos, which suggests that, by this time, commercial sea-going traffic had long been established; in fact, alabaster vases bearing Egyptian royal cartouches of the Second Dynasty have been found in Byblos. Nor were these Fourth Dynasty ships mere boats; the Palermo Stone reveals that the wood carried was for the construction of three ships each 170 feet long. The*

actual ship which was built of Phoenician cedar for Khufu, the Cheops of pyramid fame, who followed Shefru, was found in 1954. The wood was probably exported from Byblos, which seems to have been the earliest of the Phoenician cities to have developed and, from early dynastic times, to have had very close links with Egypt." (Wiseman, *Peoples of Old Testament Times*, p. 264-265)

"Phoenician sailing expertise is well indicated by the feat whereby, at the command of Pharoah Necho, they circumnavigated the whole of Africa c. 600 B.C., traveling three years for the voyage. Later, (c. 450) sailors from the Tyrian colony of Carthage sailed as far as Britain under Admiral Hamilco, probably testing the practicability of a sea route to come by Cornish tin. A little later again, Hanno sailed from Carthage down the west coast of Africa, maybe as far as the Niger, and when he got back he wrote an account of his voyage which was inscribed in the temple of Aa'al Hammon. A somewhat garbled Greek version is still extant. Madeira and the Azores may have been discovered by accident, but the alleged discovery of an authentic Phoenician inscription at Paraibo in Brazil is still regarded with skepticism." (Wiseman, p. 277-278)

Herm raises the theory that the colonies of the Tarshish merchants may have included some in the Americas.

"Before doing so, they (the Phoenicians) would have passed through the Straits of

Gibraltar, and seen that beyond it stretched another endless ocean, far more stormy than the one they knew, and moved by tides. This was a phenomenon which also amazed Alexander the Great in India centuries later. There were no tides in the Mediterranean. How the Phoenicians reacted is not recorded. They appear to have simply grown accustomed to the fact and were soon feeling their way down the Atlantic coast of Africa. According to as yet unconfirmed theories, they then even veered westward and sailed as far as America. Professor Cyrus H. Gordon of Brandeis University in Boston, at any rate, put forward the supposition that the Melungeons, a light-skinned Indian tribe in East Tennessee came, as they themselves believe from Phoenicia. Two and a half millennia before Columbus, these ancestors of theirs landed on the shores of the New World and became settlers there. Anyone who has studied the Tyrians and their voyages for any length of time will be inclined to think that this theory is likely. They were an amazing people. The things they have not recounted would fill at least as many volumes as all that the Greeks have told so volubly." (Herm, p. 137-138)

Perhaps when Herm did his research, the amazing discoveries of Professor Barry Fell of Harvard were not yet published. But in 1976, Fell's book, *America B.C.*, which was the basis of the lead article in the February, 1977, *Reader's Digest*, settled once and for all the fact that the colonies of Tarshish included many in what is now the United States!

Professor Fell's Discoveries

Perhaps the most important archaeological find

made public in recent years which helps identify the nations in Ezekiel's prophecy has been disclosed by Professor Barry Fell *(America B.C.)*. This very scholarly and highly technical volume records a multitude of discoveries which prove that the many hitherto mysterious inscriptions discovered in the Americas are actually traceable to a thousand years of commerce by sea between Tarshish in Spain and the various Phoenician colonies in *what is now the United States*. The reader is urged to obtain and study for himself these proofs of the history of the ancient settlers in the New World. Dr. Fell tells of them in terms of a very busy commercial colonization and trade, as follows:

> *"In the wake of the Celtic pioneers came the Phoenician traders of Spain, men from Cadiz who spoke the punic tongue, but wrote it in the peculiar style of lettering known as Iberian script. Although some of these traders seem to have settled only on the coast, and then only temporarily, leaving a few engraved stones to mark their visits or record their claims of territorial annexation, other Phoenicians remained here and, together with Egyptian miners, became part of the Wabanaki tribe of New England. Further south, Basque sailors came to Pennsylvania and established a temporary settlement there, leaving however no substantial monuments other than grave markers bearing their names. Further south still, Libyan and Egyptian mariners entered the Mississippi from the Gulf of Mexico, penetrating to Iowa and the Dakotas, and westward along the Arkansas and Cimarron Rivers, to leave behind inscribed records of their presence. Norse and*

> *Basque visitors reached the Gulf of St. Law-*
> *rence, introducing various mariner's terms into*
> *the language of the northern Algonquian*
> *Indians. Descendants of these visitors are also*
> *to be found apparently among the Amerindian*
> *tribes, several of which employ dialects derived*
> *in part from the ancient tongues of Phoenicia*
> *and North Africa."* (Fell, p. 7)

↪ One of Fell's most thrilling discoveries, as it bears
upon this study, is that of inscriptions which mention
Tarshish by name. In his chapter entitled "Ships of
Tarshish," Fell observes:

> *"By the eighth century B.C., a group of Syrian*
> *colonists had settled the lower reaches of the*
> *valley of the Guadalquivir River in Andalusia,*
> *southwestern Spain, where they were engaged in*
> *trading for metals mined by the natives, who*
> *seem to have been mainly Basques. Eventually*
> *invading bands of Celts in ever-increasing*
> *numbers came down from the north, and by 500*
> *B.C. they had overrun the whole region. There-*
> *after we hear no more of Phoenicians in this part*
> *of Andalusia. Now, however, we have found*
> *their inscriptions in America.*
>
> *"The alphabet has been deciphered in part by*
> *Spanish epigraphers, and most of the residual*
> *letters have now been assigned their phonetic*
> *values as a result of the discovery of Tartessian*
> *inscriptions in Central and North America. The*
> *language can now be read with relative ease, for*
> *it proves to be no more than a dialectal variant*
> *of Phoenician. In fact, one wonders why the*
> *Tartessians bothered to devise their own script,*
> *seeing they could equally well have employed*
> *the script of Phoenicia itself.*

> *"From the Bible we learn that the ships of Tarshish were the largest sea-going vessels known to the Semitic world, and the name was eventually applied to any large ocean-going vessel. On the coasts of Palestine, where the ancient psalmists of Israel could watch the vessels of their Phoenician cousins plying their trade with Lebanon and Egypt, the ships of Tarshish became proverbial as an expression of sea power.*
>
> *"Tarshish was ruled by kings, as we learn from Psalm 72, kings of comparable power to those who ruled over Sheba, since both are mentioned in the same breath, and grouped with the princes of the isles, by which is probably meant the Phoenician kings of Cyprus and Sardinia.*
>
> *"Tartessian vessels would surely have played a major role in the Celtic migration to New England."* (Fell, p. 93)

The finding of the Tarshish inscription itself is related by Dr. Fell:

> *"It was not until 1975 that Pearson's original unretouched photograph came to my notice through the courtesy of James Whittall. Some months later at Union, New Hampshire, another inscription was discovered with excellently preserved Tartessian letters, and it then became clear that the Mount Hope inscription is also written in this style, though somewhat damaged by time, vandals and erosion. Under the outline carving of a hull appears a single line of Tartessian Punic, reading from right to left, to yield: VOYAGERS FROM TARSHISH THIS STONE PROCLAIMS.*

> *"The script cannot of itself be accurately dated, but a likely estimate would perhaps be about 700 or 600 B.C. The voyagers were probably not explorers but rather merchants trading with the New England Celts who, by that date, would already be well-established fur trappers, and very likely also mining precious metals on those sites where ancient workings have been discovered."* (Fell, p. 100)

The fate of some of the ships of Tarshish is postulated by Dr. Fell with the suggestion that they could still be found:

> *"What, then, became of the many ships of Tarshish that once frequented these same coasts from two thousand to three thousand years ago? Certainly some, probably many, must also lie on the bottom, for sea travel was more dangerous in ancient times, and the storm waves could surely wreak more havoc upon the timbered hulls of Phoenician galleys than on the steel plates of modern ships."*

Fell agrees with Herm and Wiseman as to the large size and seaworthiness of the Tarshish ships:

> *"As to the relative sizes and strengths of ancient ships in comparison with those used by Columbus, medieval Europe of 1492 was in a stage of nautical skill that the ancients would have regarded as benighted. Columbus' whole expedition could mount only eighty-eight men, carried on three vessels of which two were only fifty feet in length, about the size of a small Boston fish boat. Contrast that with the Pharaohs of the Ramesside dynasty, 1200 B.C.,*

> *who could mount expeditions of ten thousand miners across the Indian Oceon to the gold-bearing lands of South Africa and Sumatra. Julius Caesar's triremes carried two hundred men, yet he found his ships outmatched in size, height and seaworthiness by those of the maritime Celts."* (Fell, p. 110)

The Celts who succeeded the Phoenicians trading with the Americas lost their fleet to Julius Caesar in 55 B.C. and with Roman conquest of Western Europe, the trading practices of the Celts with the Americas ceased and within two centuries was forgotten. Fell explains:

> *"The entire Celtic fleet was destroyed or captured while the Romans still had eighty serviceable ships, with which Caesar later, in September of 55 B.C., carried the war across the Channel to Britannia.*
>
> *"There is no further mention of British or Gaulish naval vessels in Caesar's commentaries, nor does Tacitus in the century that followed give any space or consideration to native naval might. It seems that the battle against the Veneti was the end of Celtic sea power in classical times. Except for periodic truculence by British chiefs against Roman economic exploitation, for the most part the Celtic aristocracy willingly adopted Roman manners and luxury under the sweet persuasion of competent governors; and so the Celtic lands settled down to four centuries of relative prosperity and peace. By the time the Saxon pirates appeared off their eastern coasts, the Britons had forgotten their seamanship as well as most*

*of their martial arts, and ruin soon followed,
ushering in four more centuries of ignorance
and misery."* (Fell, p. 120)

Fell leaves no room for doubt about the fact of the
merchants of Tarshish having established trading
colonies in North America.

> *"The men of Tarshish established colonies in
> eastern North America, the settlers probably
> drawn from the native Iberians (that is, Celts
> and Basques) of the Guadalquivir valley in
> Andalusia.*
>
> *"The first authenticated find of an engraved
> Phoenician tablet in an American archaelogical
> context was that of a Tartessian inscription
> found in 1938. This tablet was excavated from a
> burial chamber found at the base of Mammoth
> mound in Moundsville, West Virginia.
> Although the Tartessian alphabet had not then
> been deciphered, the similarity of the inscription
> to Iberian writing was recognized, and in the
> contemporary reports of the dig, the mound and
> its contents were attributed to European visi-
> tors. Man-made burial mounds, or tumuli, are
> characteristic of many royal graves of the Euro-
> pean Bronze Age.*
>
> *"The notion that Europeans had visited and
> even settled in North America in ancient times
> continued as an acceptable hypothesis in the
> archaelogical periodicals for the ensuing forty
> years. Then, sometime around 1870, the
> opinion became widespread that there had been
> no such callers before Columbus. The Mounds-
> ville tablet was forgotten, or dismissed as a later
> intrusion that had accidentally fallen into the*

*mound, or been surreptiously introduced by
some irresponsible person."* (Fell, p. 157)

The Phoenicians of Tarshish, says Dr. Fell, pene-
trated deep within the American continent, following
the Mississippi up to what is now Davenport, Iowa.

*"But it seems clear that Iberian and Punic-
speakers were living in Iowa in the ninth century
B.C., making use of a stone calendar regulator
whose Egyptian hieroglyphs could apparently
be read. The settlers had presumably sailed up
the Mississippi River to colonize the Davenport
area."* (Fell, p. 268)

In conclusion, Fell offers the following summary:

*"Various peoples from Europe and from
northwest Africa sailed to America three thousand years ago and established colonies here.
The primary evidence rests in the structures they
built and in the inscriptions they wrote in letters
that we now can identify as spelling phrases and
sentences whose meaning we can grasp.*

*"The decipherments point to Iberia as the
principal homeland of most of the wanderers
who found their way to America in the millennium before Christ."* (Fell, p. 289)

In the light of such conclusive scholarship, coming
to light most significantly at this time when the
nations indicated by Ezekiel to be involved in a great
Middle Eastern war, we can now say with definite
assurance that the merchants of Tarshish and "the
young lions (colonies) thereof" must include the
Western nations of Europe and the Americas, particularly the United States.

The fact that Israel's foreign minister Moshe Dayan has recently offered the United States military bases in Israel cannot be without great significance.

We hesitate to offer further conclusions. But if Ezekiel's prophecy is divinely given, and if we are to play fair with his time indications, we have little choice but to conclude that Ezekiel foresaw actions by nations which in his time bore the titles, or were known then as "merchants of Tarshish" and "the young lions thereof." They are to be involved in confrontation with the Eastern European (Communist bloc) invaders of the Middle East. This is certainly reasonable to be possible in the not-too-distant future. Ezekiel's prophecy, which he claimed was given him from God, seems to indicate that this is exactly what will take place.

Because the outcome of this war will create great change in the balance of power and cause enormous international turmoil, it will reasonably give rise to a United Europe, formed by the diabolical statesmanship of the man known in the Scripture as the Antichrist.

CHAPTER 8

Master of Deceit

As Christ is "the Truth," so the Antichrist is "the Lie." The devil is a liar and the father of lies. As we have seen, the devil gives the Antichrist power and position and imparts to him the technique of the "big lie," that he, the Antichrist, is God and is to be worshiped. The Antichrist will be known by his mastery of this policy.

The very nature of the Antichrist is deceptive since he is a false Christ or messiah. He also traffics with the demonic world, which is a world of deception as John tells us.

> "And I saw three unclean spirits like frogs come out of the mouth of the dragon, and out of the mouth of the beast, and out of the mouth of the false prophet. For they are the spirits of devils" (Rev. 16:13-14).

The Antichrist is the emissary of Satan, the arch-deceiver, and hence is also a deceiver himself.

> "And the great dragon was cast out, that old

serpent, called the Devil, and Satan, which deceiveth the whole world" (Rev. 12:9).

The Antichrist is described as using crafty deceit as a policy.

"And through his policy also he shall cause craft to prosper in his hand" (Dan. 8:25).

Thus, the Antichrist is the arch-deceiver of all time.

We should not be surprised at the totally dishonest claims and arguments put forth by the movements and human representatives of the Antichrist, which are already in the world preparing mankind and society for the great deception to come.

Since the world began, many politicians have used deceit. In this the Antichrist is not unique, except that it must be obvious that to gain allegiance from so many people, he will use claims and deceptive promises of "a better world, a world free from the harmful presence of Christians who are enemies of the state, true progress and prosperity."

To see this type of demagogy, simply look at Russia. There the press is entirely controlled for the benefit of the Communist Party, and religion is considered the opiate of the people. Russia and all communist countries are places where the movement and spirit of antichrist have already gained control, so we should have no great difficulty envisioning the demagogy of the Antichrist himself.

How Will He Deceive?

1. Through Hallucinating Drugs

As previously noted, there is much reason to believe that the power of "enchantment by the use of drugs" will be used by the Antichrist (Rev. 18:23) to help deceive all nations. A drug-crazed world would be easy to deceive.

2. Through Terror

There must also be the use of terror to deceive and coerce. Terror plays upon the imagination to bend the will with a minimum employment of actual killing. Lenin, in his own handwriting, inserted into the Soviet constitution that "terror was to be a policy of state." The Antichrist will use the fear of execution for those who do not worship his image (or bow to the state as it is embodied in him, the symbol of whom is the "image").

He will terrorize through starvation, by denying the opportunity of working, buying or selling to those who will not take his mark upon their bodies. Strictly speaking, terror is not deception, for the threat is very real. But like deception, terror is a psychological weapon.

He will use the deception of peace alternated with the threat of war in the typically communist dialectic of terror. "By peace he shall destroy many," Daniel wrote. Paradoxically, the Antichrist will be involved in many wars. "Who is like unto the beast? who is able to make war with him?" (Rev. 13:4) the nations will ask.

3. Through Political Deception

The Antichrist, like Judas Iscariot, is not really concerned with helping the poor, but is a thief who uses human misery as a ladder to gain power. This is the fundamental nature of all communism and social-ism. Well did J. Edgar Hoover label communists as "masters of deceit," and communism is setting a pattern for the empire of the Antichrist.

The Antichrist will corrupt people.

> *"And such as do wickedly against the covenant shall he corrupt by flatteries" (Dan. 11:32).*

He will gain Power by lies and flatteries.

> *". . . but he shall come in peaceably, and obtain the kingdom by flatteries" (Dan. 11:21).*

He will break truces and treaties in the manner of Stalin who said, "Promises are like pie crust, made to be broken."

> *"And after the league made with him he shall work deceitfully; for he shall come up, and shall become strong with a small people" (Dan. 11:23).*

He will use bribery to gain allies.

> *"He shall enter peaceably even upon the fattest places of the province. . . he shall scatter among them the prey, and spoil, and riches: yea, and he shall forecast his devices against the strongholds, even for a time" (Dan. 11:24).*

The words, "Scatter among them the prey and spoil," etc., refer to plunder, paid as bribes to those who do his bidding.

4. Through Religious Deception

It should never be forgotten that behind the Antichrist is Satan, who desires to be worshiped as the prince of the world in defiance against God. Hence, his servant, the Antichrist, will use religion and play deceitfully upon the religious nature of man.

Already the movements of the Antichrist, which are preparing the world for the great religious deception of the false messiah, are busy deceiving the people in the name of religion. They turn from the gospel of Christ to the false gospel of social reform. They call it the "social gospel," but it always comes out as some form of socialism. They claim to be "Christians," but in reality they depart from historic Christianity completely.

Some professors in religious colleges and seminaries turn students from faith in Christ to no faith, and then to the "improvement (socialization) of society as a substitute for Christian faith. An example of the use of religion to help further the Antichrist's kingdom is found in the behavior of the World Council of Churches. The following news account is illustrative:

> "What is strange and terrible is that an international religious organization, with 263 member churches, is in the business of supplying money to terrorist groups. This has been going on since 1969 when the World Council of Churches created its Special Fund at a meeting held in London under the chairmanship of U.S. Senator George McGovern, who was participating in his role as a church layman.
>
> "The first detailed documentation of the WCC's funding of terrorist groups appeared in **The Reader's Digest** in 1971. That article revealed the WCC was giving aid to nineteen revolutionary groups! 'Worse,' said the magazine, 'Four of the most generously financed groups are avowedly communist. At least three

of the four, according to the London Institute for the Study of Conflict, are receiving arms from the Soviet Union. All four have records of bloody terrorism, not only against whites, but against those black Africans who repudiate their terrorist methods.'

"*Yet the record shows that the WCC, instead of halting assistance to revolutionary groups, voted in August, 1972, to increase the fund to one million dollars.*

"*Moreover, the WCC example apparently has led other church organizations to take up the cause of the terrorists.* **Christian Challenge** *magazine reported in its October issue that the Foundation for Community Organization (IFCO), which has its headquarters in the National Council of Churches building in New York City, recently made grants to the Mozambique Liberation Front and the Zimbabwe African National Union. According to* **Christian Challenge,** *the Episcopal Church has been the 'largest single contributor to IFCO.'*

"*It was demonstrated anew after the 1972 U.S. presidential election, when the new general secretary of the WCC, Rev. Philip Potter of the West Indies Island of Dominica, attacked the United States for its role in Southeast Asia. Dr. Potter said: 'We have read with horror of the massive airlift of weapons of war into South Vietnam by the United States and . . . the heaviest bombing yet, with subsequent killing and maiming of people and the destruction of the Indochinese countryside.' He called on President Nixon to withdraw 'all your military forces.'*

> *"Dr. Potter didn't have a word of criticism for the North Vietnamese. He didn't say a word about the terrorism practiced by Hanoi's forces or about the occupation of South Vietnamese territory by communist troops. But, then, that's the way the way the WCC has operated for years. It never finds anything to criticize in the doings of revolutionary states. In fact, the WCC pours money into the hands of terrorist leaders.*
>
> *"It is important the public understand the WCC's record and role. The World Council should be seen for what it is—a propaganda and financial aid arm for revolutionary movements." (The Ledger,* Montrose, CA, Feb., 1973).

↩ To further illustrate the church's trend toward apostasy, consider a book published in July, 1977, *The Myth of God Incarnate.* This gem of apostasy was written by six prominent Anglican theologians who decided to "update" the Bible in this age of science and remove any vestige of the deity of Jesus.

Furthermore, a news service reported in September, 1977, that a number of scholars and professors from some outstanding American seminaries are seriously questioning the deity of Jesus Christ, bemoaning their past "error" of teaching Jesus as the Son of God.

It seems that many hitherto orthodox mainline denominations are also jumping on the bandwagon. In a scathing rebuke of a book edited by a former Episcopalian bishop and made possible by a grant from the Episcopal Church Publishing Company, the Rev. Jerome F. Politzer charged that this book "skillfully weaves together the latest themes in liberation theology with Marxist analysis of the

prevailing economic and political system in the
United States."

> *" 'It paints the American way of life in such a
> fashion that one is led to believe that the
> economic structures of our national life are the
> next thing to the kingdom of sin, Satan and
> death.' In contrasts, Marxist systems are pre-
> sented as 'being close to the fulfillment of the
> Kingdom of God on earth.' "* (The Wanderer,
> Aug. 25, 1977)

The 189th General Assembly of the United Presbyterian Church, which met in the summer of 1977,
wholeheartedly embraced the Confession of 1967, a
document which has eliminated the Westminster
Confession of Faith, a fundamentalist view of the
Holy Scriptures. Thus, the largest Presbyterian
denomination has officially moved away from orthodoxy and has placed its emphasis on a theology of
liberalism.

An amendment specifying that no funds of the
General Assembly could be used to support organizations "which used violence for social change" was
rejected!

And to top it off, a Czech Communist, Dr. Vaclav
Kejr, "preached" the ecumenical service at the
General Assembly! (*Christian Beacon,* July 7,
1977)

On the Catholic front, there appeared in the
National Jesuit News a document entitled, "Nation-
al Planning and the Need for a Revolutionary Social
Strategy: A Christian-Maoist Perspective." *(The
Rising Tide,* p. 97, July 18, 1977)

Had enough? Here's one more. In the summer of
1977, the National Council of Churches proudly

announced its contribution of bringing sexual equality closer to fulfillment. Alleging that the Bible is the main source of sexism, twenty-four Council scholars said they are planning to rewrite the Revised Standard Version to eliminate as many references to "man" or "he" or "him" as they deem necessary.

Denying the truth of such fundamental doctrines as the incarnation of Jesus Christ, religious agents of Antichrist deceive the people in order to prepare the way for the worship of the Antichrist.

When all real Christians, the true Church, and the presence of the Holy Spirit are removed from the earth by the parousia (the second coming of Christ), there will henceforth be no resistive hindrance to the full realization of the kingdom of the Antichrist, which will be backed by apostate Christianity and other religions. St. Paul clearly warned of this:

> *"Let no man deceive you by any means: for that day shall not come, except there come a falling away first, and that man of sin be revealed, the son of perdition; Who opposeth and exalteth himself above all that is called God, or that is worshipped; so that he, as God sitteth in the temple of God, shewing himself that he is God" (II Thes. 2:3-4).*

In what specific ways will the Antichrist deceive through religion and take advantage of apostasy?

1. He will deny the reality of God and the deity of Jesus Christ.

> *"He is antichrist, that denieth the Father and the Son" (I John 2:22).*

2. Like these forerunners before him, he will with

unashamed blatancy, deny the second coming of
Christ in the flesh.

> *"For many deceivers are entered into the*
> *world, who confess not Jesus Christ is come in*
> *the flesh " (II John 7). The correct Greek*
> *translation of II John 7 is, "is coming."*

3. The Antichrist will also receive the status of
God and be worshiped as a result of a miraculous
healing.

> *"And I saw. . . (the beast) as it were wounded*
> *to death; and his deadly wound was healed: and*
> *all the world wondered after the beast" (Rev.*
> *13:3).*

4. Using false and apostate religion to help him
come to power, the Antichrist will ally himself with
the head of all apostate and pagan religious organizations and destroy them. Thus he will wipe out all
vestiges of religion, especially as they are found in
Rome, the capital city of the False Prophet. The
False Prophet will, however, himself escape the
destruction launched by this cohort, the Antichrist.

> *". . . these shall hate the whore (i.e., apostate*
> *Rome), and shall make her desolate and naked,*
> *and shall eat her flesh, and burn her with fire"*
> *(Rev. 17:16).*

At the time John wrote, this city was Rome. In the
last days it will probably again be Rome, since
Scripture is consistent in its identification.

Astonishingly, even in the headquarters city of
Apostate religion some true believers will still be left.
They are advised to flee the soon-coming destruction

of this capital of religious deceit: "And I heard another voice from heaven, saying, Come out of her, my people" (Rev. 18:4).

The beast shall see the end of his religious deceptions at the Battle of Armageddon after which he shall be confined to the bottomless pit.

"And the beast was taken, and with him the false prophet that wrought miracles before him, with which he deceived them that had received the mark of the beast. . ...These both were cast alive into a lake of fire burning with brimstone" *(Rev. 19:20).*

Thus the deception of the last days, political and religious, shall come to its proper end. In the meantime, we should never overlook for a moment the continuing policy of deception which is the hallmark of the movements of the Antichrist, even now in the world. These activities should be exposed and opposed by all true believers in Jesus Christ.

CHAPTER 9

An Empire Restored

In 1922, Benito Mussolini, then an obscure editor of a socialist newspaper, led a revolution in Italy which was ruled by a weak government and beset by economic stagnation following World War I. His new form of government was called "fascism," after the "fasces," the symbol of the lictor of ancient Roman cities. This new movement was also known as "National Socialism" and had as its goal the extension of Italian power and the resurrection and revival of the Roman Empire.

Mussolini's attempts at latter day Roman imperialism laid the groundwork for the rise of Adolf Hitler and almost destroyed the world. World War II became inevitable because of the policies of these two types of fascism. But Mussolini lacked the character and Italy lacked the martial spirit to bring about his announced goals. He became known as "The Sawdust Caesar," the shadow of Hitler who was far more a Caesar than his mentor.

For a time Mussolini's posturings gave rise to the

suspicion that the biblical prophecies concerning a revival of the Roman empire, as predicted in Daniel, would then come to pass. This notion faded with the destruction of the Third Reich and fascism in Italy. Recently, however, it has again become a possibility in the establishment of the European Common Market.

The emphasis upon the economic nature of the Common Market has revealed the need for European unity in marketing, but in it are also the seeds of a political unity of Europe. Europe in the past has, through its stronger states, been a center of imperialism throughout the world. At one time the British Empire was the largest in history. Spain, France, Germany and Holland also possessed large empires. Now all are gone with the winds of anti-imperialism which have reduced every empire but the Soviet Union.

The disunity and provincialism of Europe has held this mighty continent of productive and talented people back from their potential destiny. Nationalism has been too important, and language barriers and political rivalries have crippled them. Great wars between European countries have crippled virtually the whole world at times. Today the spectre of communism has divided each European country and serves to further prevent even an economic unity based upon the Common Market concept.

Given today's rapid transportation and communication, a United States of Europe is eminently feasible, and if successful, would make it the mightiest nation on earth. Several attempts to unite Europe by conquest and force of arms, notably by Adolf Hitler in this century, have failed. Not since the Holy Roman Empire and more effectively before that in

the days of imperial Rome, has European hegemony
been attempted with any success.

Today the need for unity is present, but European
nations continue to consider themselves as countries
rather than states in a great European nation. Nothing presently in prospect seems to offer the motivation which would attract or force Europe into one
nation.

But the Bible indicates this will change someday,
perhaps even more swiftly than people can imagine.

A Shift of Power

The great unleashing of what will amount to World
War III will come, as previously shown, according to
the prophecy of Ezekiel 38-39, and will involve
Western Europe in the conflict when Eastern
Europe, led by Russia, moves to seize the oil fields of
the Middle East.

As we have demonstrated, Western Europe is
extremely vulnerable to the loss of Middle Eastern
petroleum. It also faces Soviet expansionism.
Europe is incapable at present, and will be for the
forseeable future, of doing much more about Russia's
invasion than protest. But the given possibility of this
seizure will doubtless do by fear what economics and
common sense have been unable to do hitherto. Out
of the Russian-led invasion, Europe, it seems likely,
will finally unite and form a nation strong enough to
insure economic security and political strength.

This seems clear but it also seems highly unlikely,
given present circumstances. Nevertheless, it is an
obvious move in the light of what is coming.

If Russia is defeated and drastically reduced as a
world power; if, as the Bible indicates, part of
Eastern Europe is in ruins as the result of a nuclear
attack, as Ezekiel's predictions hint; then there will

be only two world powers left, the United States and a disciplined, emerging Red China.

Europe will fear economic imperialism by the United States and, if famine should threaten the Far East, will fear the military might of a hungry China with its hordes of soldiers whose Communist masters will not hesitate to sacrifice them by the millions if they are sufficiently motivated. Doubtless Communists within Europe itself will still be around to remind Europeans what it almost did.

This is the real prospect which will demonstrate to a frightened Europe that it must unite. Only if it is united, armed and working as one great nation can it become a world power to prevent the resurgence of communism or the attempt at global conquest by Red China.

The Antichrist will be the catalyst and leader of this new Europe. He will come from one of the nations which was part of the old Roman Empire and will wage small wars of conquest, and then by a satanically inspired series of brilliant political maneuvers, forge again the equivalent of a united Europe. From that base he will impose a peace upon the Middle East and move toward world government, utilizing war, peace, deceit and his own tremendous personality to bring it about.

Europe, his base of operations, is therefore destined to rise again to world prominence and power. The utter practicality of this scenario is now visible both from a scriptural reference and political realism. In a word, it is a workable scheme. The predictions of the Bible are now clearly understandable.

The Move Is On

Europe is rife with godlessness and unbelief. Huge

new suburbs without churches are being built around its cities. The religion of the past is losing its hold. Europe is fiercely devoted to pleasure, productivity and profit. It is ripe for a leader, given the very real threat which is now posed by Soviet imperialism. Far more dependent upon Mideast oil than the United States, Europe is always within days of running out of petroleum—it produces little of its own—yet its whole system is based upon petroleum. Always the sword of scarcity hangs over Europe, suspended by a very thin string. When threatened, she will unite as a restored Roman Empire, ready to play out the last themes of time.

There are four different and separate strands of biblical knowledge and predictions concerning the revival of a "Romanized" Europe in the last days. We get the whole picture when these four strands come together: Daniel's vision of the image (Dan. 2:31-45); Daniel's vision of the four beasts (Dan. 7:1-27; 8:3-25) (Here the area from which the Antichrist will come is described as being part of both the ancient Greek and Roman empires which were in many places co-mingled.); St. John's vision of the beast from the sea (Rev. 13:1-7); St. John's vision of the doom of "Babylon," i.e., Rome (Rev. 17:1-6, 9-18;; 18:1-2, 9, 10, 20, 21, 23, 24).

All of these visions from the most detailed prophetic portions of Daniel and The Revelation clearly implicate Rome. For Daniel, Rome was not yet a clear, present reality except prophetically, since he lived during the early days of the Roman Republic. Nevertheless, he was granted visions which predicted both ancient, imperial Rome and the revival of the Roman Empire in the last days. This is abundantly clear and plain in his writings.

St. John, who lived during the zenith of Rome's imperial power, could see more clearly the nature of Daniel's prophecy concerning Rome, upon which his own seem to have been projected, only more fully.

John used the term "Babylon" to stand for Rome because his book would come under the scrutiny of the Roman police authorities by whom the early Christians, even in John's time, had already suffered much. But he clearly indicated that Babylon stood for Rome in Revelation 17:9 where he identifies the seven hills of Rome. Babylon itself is a mystery (Rev. 17:5) as "that great city *which reigneth over the kings of the earth*" (Rev. 17:18). At the time John wrote, he could have meant only Rome.

CHAPTER 10

A God Created

We must first distinguish between the "personal" religion of the Antichrist himself and the religion he cynically espouses and promotes. He has no true, personal religion, for as we have seen, he denies the Father and the Son.

1. We will honor the god of forces:

> *"But in this estate shall he honor the God of forces; and a god whom his fathers knew not shall he honour with gold, and silver, and with precious stones, and pleasant things" (Dan. 11:38).*

2. He will "worship" Satan. As Satan offered Jesus Christ the kingdoms of this world, so Satan will offer them to the Antichrist.

> *"And the devil, taking him (Jesus) up into an high mountain, shewed unto him all the kingdoms of the world in a moment of time. And the devil said unto him, All this power will I give*

108

thee, and the glory of them; for that is delivered unto me; and to whosoever I will give it. If thou therefore wilt worship me, all shall be thine" (Luke 4:5-7).

Jesus refused this offer. On the contrary, however, the Antichrist will accept it, receiving from the dragon his "power, and his seat, and great authority" (Rev. 13:2).

3. He also "worships" himself.

". . . who opposeth and exalteth himself above all that is called God, or that is worshipped; so that he as God sitteth in the temple of God, showing himself that he is God" (II Thess. 2:4).

The "religion" the Antichrist espouses and promotes is the blasphemous worship of himself, conducted by the False Prophet, the leader of world apostate and idolatrous religion. The False Prophet's role is multi-faceted.

He is to bend the religious sentiment of mankind toward acceptance of the false Christ, the "new" messiah.

"And I beheld another beast (the False Prophet). . . (who) causeth the earth and them which dwell therein to worship the first beast, whose deadly wound was healed" (Rev. 13:11, 12).

The purpose of the Antichrist's religion, led by the False Prophet, will be to harness man's religious nature, thus strengthening his rule. This will assure that all social groups and forces are subservient to the Antichrist's authority.

By heading the consolidation of apostate religion, the False Prophet will satisfy the religious nature of people who have rejected Christ and God, but still have need to worship someone or something.

The False Prophet is the spirit of Satan in clerical robes; he has "two horns" (religious powers) and speaks "like a dragon" with satanic mouthings.

Thus he is the powerful head of all the apostate and pagan religions of the world. The two horns may speak of both civil and religious authority, or may represent apostate "Christianity," apostate Judaism and the pagan religions.

By promoting worship of the Antichrist, the political leader, the False Prophet will cause a union of "church" and state with the "church" subservient to the state. This is why ecumenical church union movements are to be opposed when they involve apostate "Christians." This movement is preparing the world for the Antichrist, the False Prophet and the one-church religious order.

It should not seem remarkable that apostate Christianity today is not opposed to anti-Christian communism. As we have seen, it is already making alliances with it. God's message to apostate Christianity in its organized form is:

> *"Whosoever transgresseth and abideth not in the doctrine of Christ, hath not God. . . If there come any unto you, and bring not this doctrine, receive him not into your house, neither bid him God speed" (II John 9, 10).*

The point that John makes is that any union between the church and apostates is reprehensible.

The False Prophet, as a counterfeit of the Holy Spirit who draws people to Christ, will eventually cause the world to worship Satan, the god of this world. That worship is Satan's ultimate aim. The basic sin of Satan is a desire to be worshiped instead of God, who banished him from heaven and his place as the mightiest of angels.

Note that Satan wishes to counterfeit God; the Antichrist wishes to counterfeit Christ; and the False Prophet wishes to counterfeit the Holy Spirit—thus making themselves "the unholy trinity." How far their counterfeiting will go!

Furthermore, to symbolize each person's willingness to obey and worship the Antichrist, the False Prophet will direct the worship of mankind toward an "image" of the Antichrist.

> "... *saying to them that dwell on the earth, that they should make an image to the beast, which had the wound by a sword, and did live*" (Rev. 13:14).

The image of the beast may be a poster image, as in Red China, where people used to pray to photographs or paintings of Mao Tse-Tung, and confess their "sins" to it. This is not an overstatement. Such practices have been clearly photographed and described in the official *Red China Pictorial Review*.

Or, the image could be statues like those of Lenin now standing in Russia. Everywhere in the two communist countries, "Big brother is watching you."

Or, the image could itself be telecast live over a worldwide television network via satellite. Much credence lies with this theory, since John writes:

> "*And he had power to give life unto the image of the beast, that the images of the beast should both speak, and cause that as many as would not worship the image of the beast should be killed*" (Rev. 13:15).

Perhaps most terrifying of all is the feasibility of
two-way television monitors, through which anyone
could be spied upon by a government agent. These
are already being developed in America.

It is obvious that only in the technological age of
the last half of the twentieth century can the prophecies of the Antichrist become literal happenings,
exactly as the Bible predicts! We will watch as
movements and inventions appear that make these
divinely authorized prophecies even more a possibility.

Economics of a Beast

Eventually all the nations of the world will do
away with the gold standard and conduct business by
computers which will automatically transfer funds
from one establishment to another. The book of The
Revelation describes this practice as the "mark of the
beast," an idea enforced by the False Prophet!

> *"And he causeth all, both small and great,
> rich and poor, free and bond, to receive a mark
> in their right hand, or in their foreheads: And
> that no man might buy or sell, save he that had
> the mark, or the name of the beast, or the
> number of his name" (Rev. 13:17).*

A modern method of identification being developed is the use of a "walking credit card" number
placed invisibly on the hand or forehead. These
numbers can be picked up by electronic scanners and
fed back to a computer.

One such computer, which exists in Brussels,
Belgium, is connected with over five hundred different data banks throughout the world. There are over
fifteen countries involved in this program called

"SWIFT"—the "Society for Worldwide Interbank Financial Telecommunication."

Certain proposals have already been made in the U.S. to enforce alien registration by an invisible mark upon the body!

Communism, which is an antichrist movement, is the first great power in history that openly seeks to rule the whole world. Its aim is complete control of life and the elimination of all worship of God.

Its tools of control could very easily soon be the "image of the beast," the "mark of the beast," and the use of apostate, godless religion that is already promoting socialism. As in Russia, this religion is becoming a political force, a pawn of the state. So-called "Christiana-Marxist discussion" are even now being featured in some liberal church and seminary groups in America.

Lest Christians help the movements of the Antichrist, they should study to see the evils of all forms of socialism and political ecumenicalism, and oppose them by exposure and withdrawal of support.

The Antichrist will be the greatest enemy freedom-preserving governments and economic liberty will ever know. Wherever he reigns, all liberties will be lost. Now that political freedom has finally been achieved in some countries after centuries of tyranny, how sickening today to see the trend going the other way. Yet that is happening as the way of the Antichrist is being prepared. African countries newly "liberated" from colonialism are sliding back into native totalitarianism far worse than colonialism ever was.

Latin American countries, after a brief experience in political freedom, are sinking one by one under the terrorism of new dictatorships.

How proud America was that she had bestowed liberty and a constitution upon the Philippines and preserved freedom for South Korea. But both countries, in one year, scrapped their constitutions and veered back into dictatorships, although benign.

Can we not see the trend of the times?

And what about America herself? Is freedom growing, or is government-control growing? What strange spirit possesses men who want freedom, are willing to fight and die to get it, and then meekly surrender it so soon, helpless in the face of the growing state dictatorship?

We fought World War I to "make the world safe for democracy" and to end wars. Yet Hitler rose to power and caused the greatest war ever known. After him came the terrible dictatorship of communism which now controls almost half of the people on earth.

We fought a bloody war in Korea and a worse one in Vietnam, both designed to "stop communism in Southeast Asia," yet some American young people demonstrate for communist causes, exalt communist heroes and heroines and say they "will not fight against the communist enemy" even if he should invade America (this from a report of a recent Gallup Poll).

Has the world gone mad? Has America lost her mind? Why can we no longer withstand or stop dictatorships at home or abroad?

The answer is simple. The world is building toward the welcoming of its final dictator, the Antichrist. His cause is at hand. It will ultimately prevail, and unless we re-energize our spirit as a free people, we shall lose our own country much faster than is necessary.

Let there be no mistake: the Antichrist is coming.

His agents are at hand. His followers have already landed and have taken much of the earth. His kingdom grows every day.

Yet the Antichrist can be slowed and even held at bay—perhaps for a generation—if we again return to God and once more take up the cause of freedom. But we have only a few years or months. Then the night will surely fall.

How can it be that the forces of the Antichrist are here so massively, so victoriously, so openly, and yet the world does not realize the fact? It is because it is the nature of the Antichrist to deceive. He is not only the arch-destroyer, but the arch-deceiver of all time.

People who will not see through God's eyes, who ignore God's Word, never understand even when they are told the ugly facts. The prophet Daniel wrote:

> *"But the wicked shall do wickedly: and none of the wicked shall understand; but the wise shall understand" (Dan 12:10).*

For the tirst time in history, a worldwide movement with all the characteristics of the predicted Antichrist government has appeared upon the earth. It is openly and frankly anti-Christian in every dimension. Its politics and economics are those of the great "beast" of the prophecies of Scripture. And yet despite this, life goes on as before, and the great majority of people are ignorant, uncaring and even unbelieving when they hear the truth!

Since, however, God's people are to be privileged to know the truth, let us clearly see this unmistakable kingdom of evil in order that false optimism may end and men may oppose the Antichrist and all his works. While it is day, let us labor to hold back the night.

Politically Religious

The difference between the government of the Antichrist and those of other dictators is that his government demands worship as well as total submission and obedience. Communist dictatorships are already this way in theory, and increasingly so in practice. Castro, in fact, abolished Christmas in favor of a July celebration honoring his revolution.

Through all the communist world the "new communist man" takes the place of the "new man in Christ," as taught by Christianity. Atheism is their official philosophy. In matter of fact, communism replaces the worship of God with the worship of the state and party, plus the adoration of the Communist dictator as the embodiment of the state. Note carefully the following 1968 newspaper report:

> "*HONG KONG—In China these days, there seems to be only one god and his name is Mao Tse-Tung.*
>
> "*The superhuman figure of Mao, chairman of the Chinese Communist Party, is the center of such praise and adulation, it is almost ludicrous.*
>
> "*By a rough count, the name of Chairman Mao is invoked approximately 4.5 million times each day on the airwaves of China and perhaps a hundred times as often by itinerant propagandists. Since the Great Proletarian Cultural Revolution formally began just over two years ago, over three billion sets of his writings and reproductions of his picture have been produced.*
>
> "*Miraculous tales of illnesses cured and triumphs over natural laws outnumber the*

miracles ascribed to the saints of all the re-ligions of the world. Study of Mao's canonical and sacrosanct thought enables ordinary mor-tals to perform incredible feats, while merely thinking of his name ends bodily pain and induces spiritual exaltation.

"It consequently appears that the idolization-adulation is too mild a term.

"The intensity of the deification of Mao is apparent in specific incidents and figures. In Hupei province in the north, the official press reveals:

" 'The common scene in the morning in the rural areas is "the four-firsts," that is the first act: salute Chairman Mao; the first words to utter: "Long, long life to Chairman Mao"; the first song to sing: "The East is Red"; the first thing to do: study Chairman Mao's great instructions.' "

Every day, poor and lower middle-class peasants perform the rites of "seeking advice from and making reports to " the portrait of Chariman Mao.

"Before meals, many poor and middle-class peasants chant the chairman's supreme in-structions before his portrait and salute him." (Los Angeles Times, Oct. 30, 1968)

✔ This tendency to portray a leader as savior is evidently becoming common in other parts of the world, notably in the emerging nations in Africa. Read carefully the following article by David Lamb of the *Los Angeles Times,* dated September 22, 1977, and see how closely it parallels the conditions described in the book of The Revelation at the time of the Antichrist:

> *"LOME, Togo—The first order of business when Togo's president plans a public appearance is to crank up his cheering section—one thousand dancing women who job it is to accompany the president and lavish him with songs of praise.*
>
> *"For twenty dollars Togolese can buy a wristwatch on which the illuminated portrait of President Etienne Chassingbe Eyadema fades and reappears every fifteen seconds. Eyadema recently unveiled a hugh bronze statue of himself, and an Eyadema comic book is the hottest-selling publicatioin in Lome.*
>
> *"In Zaire, the evening news begins with an image of heavenly clouds parting, and as the angelic music swells, the face of President Mobutu Sese Seko slowly fills the screen. He stares kindly at his viewers for what seems a very long time, a symbol of great wisdom and mystical strength. . .*
>
> *"The phenomenon that Zaire and Togo share—as do a good many other African countries—is presidential cultism. And although it is hardly unique to Africa, leaders here have developed the self-worship process into a fine art while bestowing upon themselves god-like qualities and the unquestioned authority of the most powerful chieftain. . .*
>
> *"Accordingly, many African presidents attach titles to their names to convey this image. Mzee, the Swahili title for Jomo Kenyatta of Kenya, translates as 'Wise Old Man'; Julius Nyerere of Tanzania is know as 'the Teacher';*

Eyadema of Togo is 'the Guide'; Felix Houphouet-Boigny of the Ivory Coast is 'the Number One Peasant'; and Macias Nguema of Equatorial Guinea is 'the National Miracle.'

"Frequently the apparent adulation surrounding the chief is spoon-fed to the public. Large crowds are ordered to gather when the presidents of Tanzania, Kenya, Zaire, and Togo make public appearances. In Kenya, the president's picture is on display in every restaurant, shop and office. In Uganda, Idi Amin, who had a second-grade education, declared himself a doctor of philosophy.

"One of the dangers of cultism is that the presidents eventually start believing they are all the things their sycophants tell them they are. They rise above criticism—often exiling or killing critics. And perhaps almost believing they are immortal, they retard the development of leadership needed to ensure a smooth transition when power eventually does change hands."

In view of the idolatry we have seen in these articles, it is essential that the religious element in the politics of Antichrist not be lost sight of in any appraisal of his government. The aim is spiritual control, and not merely political government which the Antichrist seeks. As we have seen previously, the Antichrist "shall exalt himself, and magnify himself above every god" (Dan. 11:36).

The Source of Power

After rising from the sea of nations, the Antichrist will demonstrate his governing ability among ten kings. They willingly give their power to him.

> *"And the ten horns which thou sawest are ten kings, which have received no kingdom as yet; but receive power as kings one hour with the beast. These have one mind, and shall give their power and strength unto the beast"* (Rev. 17:12, 13).

Political power will come from several sources:
Satan:

> *"And the dragon gave him his power, and his seat, and great authority"* (Rev. 13:2).

Oratory:

> *"And the beast. . . (had a). . . mouth as the mouth of a lion"* (Rev. 13:2).
> *"And there was given unto him a mouth speaking great things and blasphemies"* (Rev. 13:5).

Wisdom to solve the difficulties of nations:

> *"And in the latter time of their kingdom, when the transgressors are come to the full, a king of fierce countenance, and understanding dark sentences, shall stand up"* (Dan. 8:23).

Craftiness:

> *"And through his policy also he shall cause craft to prosper in his land"* (Dan. 8:25).

Military might:

> *"He shall subdue three kings"* (Dan. 7:24).
> *"And they worshipped the beast, saying, Who is like unto the beast? Who is able to make war with him?"* (Rev. 13:4).

The government of the Antichrist seeks total state control of all men. He comes from small beginnings, first rules but one country, then three, then ten, and then all nations.

> *"And all the world wondered after the beast. And they worshipped the dragon which gave power unto the beast: and they worshipped the beast"* (Rev. 13:3, 4).

The best description of the Antichrist's government is that it will be similar to that of a communistic, totalitarian, atheistic state in which the leader himself is the personification of the "cult of personality." He will be the most willful and lawless man of his age (II Thess. 2:8). As we have previously written, it seems likely that communism is a pattern, but the Antichrist may arise in the chaos of the destruction of the Soviet-led army and homeland, as indicated in Ezekiel 38 and 39. This would mean that people might see him at first as the best-equipped leader to thwart communism itself, though many communists will find him psychologically and politically acceptable.

Death will be the penalty for those who oppose or reject him.

> *"And he had power to . . . cause that as many would not worship the image of the beast should be killed"* (Rev. 13:15).

While the main thrust of the government of the Antichrist is political control with the ultimate aim of spiritual conquest of all men, making the earth a permanent enclave of rebellion against God, he will understand the necessity of the economic control of man as well. As we have seen, he will cause all people to receive a mark on their bodies in order to conduct business (Rev. 13:16, 17).

It is notable that communism, the greatest anti-christ movement of the ages so far, considers man primarily an economic creature. This was the view of Marx and Lenin, and it is the view of all communists today. The so-called "dictatorship of the proletariat" is only the dictatorship of the Communist Party, with the total economic power of any communist-dominated country in the hands of the party. The military might of the Soviet Union will undoubtedly someday be smashed, but the system will continue with some changes under the leadership of the Antichrist.

Economic rights do not exist in a communist land. There are no personal or property rights in a communist country. Governing Marxists recognize that, if people must work for the state which owns the means of production and distribution, they are totally at the mercy of the state, the only employer.

The Antichrist will adapt this simple but powerful tool of economic dictatorship in his march toward totalitarian control by forbidding people to engage in commerce unless they swear all allegiance to him.

Communism today, of all movements in history, most nearly fits the description of the coming rule of the Antichrist in all details. It is anti-Christian and atheistic. Politically and economically, it is an absolute dictatorship. It flourishes by deceit, ruthlessness, the cruel liquidation of all its enemies, and is anxious to eliminate the worship of God in favor of state "worship." It asks of its adherents the loyalty and submission that belongs only to the God of righteousness, and it is an unmixed evil in every respect.

It should seem evident to all Christians that the Antichrist will head a totalitarian economic, political and religious dictatorship of the left, similar to communism, based upon utter ruthlessness, death and deception. Therefore, any assistance given to those forms of government or religion which aid the progress of the leftist state is simply assistance to the forerunner of the ultimate dictatorship. Imagine the whole world in the grip of a Stalin; a merciless, all-powerful, paranoid ruler with absolute control over every phase of man's life!

CHAPTER 11

Twice Revealed

In 1970 the popular "seeress" Jeanne Dixon predicted that a child then born in Syria would be the Antichrist of Scripture. Later she said she may have been mistaken. The only conclusion we should draw from this is that the question of when the Antichrist will appear is a question coming more and more to the forefront of public interest.

In this study we shall offer detailed guidelines as to possibly when the Antichrist will appear. This will suggest an in-depth review of all that can be determined from present knowledge about the Antichrist. We fully acknowledge that no one can exhaust the Holy Scriptures, since biblical prophecies are being continually fulfilled.

However, much that is clear at this time was not only unknown but unknowable a few years ago.

Most assuredly, more information shall soon be revealed which is unknown today. This fact should remove the temptation to be dogmatic about prophecy, an all too frequent practice in other times.

In the past, Bible scholars have set forth their understanding of the Antichrist. Notably among these was Sir Robert Anderson in his book, *The Coming Prince.* This outstanding work, written before World War I and revised shortly afterward, is now, of course, outdated, so fast has been the march of prophetic fulfillment. Sir Robert foresaw even this when he wrote:

> *"Moreover in forecasting the fulfillment of these prophecies, we are dealing with events which, while they may occur within the lifetime of living men, may yet be delayed for centuries. Our part is not to prophesy, but only to interpret; and we may well rest content with the certainty that, when the Apocalyptic visions are in fact fulfilled, their fulfillment will be clear, not merely to minds educated in mysticism, but to all who are capable of observing public facts.*
>
> *"Through the gradual unfolding, it may be of influences even now in operation; or far more probably as the outcome of some great European crisis in the future, this confederation of nations shall be developed and thus the state will be prepared on which shall appear that awful being, the great leader of men in the eventful days which are to close the era of Gentile supremacy."*

More than sixty years have gone by since Sir Robert wrote about the Antichrist. During this time, four great world-changing events have come to pass, all of which were necessary in order to set the stage for the dramatic rise of the Antichrist. With the exception of the first of these listed happenings, these events could hardly have been guessed by Sir Robert. This is not his fault, it is simply the nature of prophetic predictions to be obscure until the time of fulfillment. The four great events are:

1. The regathering of Israel.
2. The emergence of world-shrinking, modern communications and transportation, making world government possible.
3. The rise of atheistic communism as a world movement, hungry to occupy the whole earth in rebellion against God, and setting a pattern for the government of the Antichrist.
4. The discovery of nuclear weapons with the potential of the mass destruction forecast in the Bible.

It would have been impossible even sixty years ago for any Bible scholar, however knowledgeable, to have foreseen the emergence and exact nature of all of these events. Yet we now know that without them the Antichrist would not come into the power the Bible says will be his.

Matthew 24 and Luke 21 contain many signs of the last days which precede the coming of Christ and herald the rise of the Antichrist. Though in isolated instances in the past, these signs may have been observable. Today they are more intense and frequent than they have ever been in previous generations. One needs only to read the daily newspaper to be aware of: "nation rising against nation, and kingdom against kingdom: . . .famines, pestilences, and earthquakes, in diverse places" (Matt. 24:7); Christians being delivered up to be afflicted and killed and hated (Matt. 24:9); "men's hearts failing them for fear and for looking toward those things which are coming on the earth" (Luke 21:26).

Jesus further warned, "But as the days of Noah were, so shall also the coming of the Son of man be" (Matt. 24:37). The days of Noah were characterized by godlessness, eating and drinking, pleasure-seeking, violence, immorality, marrying and giving in marriage. It takes little discernment to realize these are also marks of our own times.

As we have said, there will be two revealings of the Antichrist. The proofs for this have already been mentioned, but it is necessary to repeat some of the points to make further conclusions.

Christian Insight

As we have seen, long before the Antichrist is openly revealed to the whole world, he will probably be clearly known to those Christians who know the Scriptures and are studying the signs of the times. Daniel 12:10 states this: "None of the wicked shall understand; but the wise shall understand."

We have also seen many identifying marks of the Antichrist. We must repeat six of these which will become increasingly clear as time passes:

1. He will "come up strong with a small people," emerging from some division of the ancient Greek Empire of Alexander, which is also the Roman Empire. He will plunder his way to power by taking property from the "haves" and giving it to the "have nots." Hence, he will be a socialist.

2. He will head a mighty army and be victorious in war.

3. He will make a covenant of peace with re-gathered Israel, and at the mid-point will forsake this agreement.

4. He will form an international alliance of great political power.

5. He will be an atheist personally, though he will ally himself with organized apostate religion headed by the False Prophet.

6. He will deceive through his use of "peace propaganda." Our age is notorious for its abundance of peace groups which shout for peace while simultaneously breeding hatred and violence.

"For when they shall say, Peace and safety; then sudden destruction cometh upon them" (I Thess. 5:3).

What significant developments should we watch for as we near the Antichrist's revelation to Christians? We suggest a possible order of their appearance, though some of them may appear simultaneously.

1. The rapid rise and success of organized apostasy in a worldwide super "church" or united ecclesiastical organization similar to the apostate World Council of Churches; the apostasy of which St. Paul warns as taking place before the parousia. It is necessary to set the stage for the rise of the False Prophet, the partner-in-crime of the Antichrist.

Without the general apostasy, there could be no False Prophet, no universal religious organization, or worship of the image of the beast.

2. The Russian invasion of the Middle East described in Ezekiel 38-39 must come to create the conditions of the covenant between the beast and Israel.

Note very carefully that there is no reference to the beast, the False Prophet, or the return of glory of Jesus in the battle described in Ezekiel 38-39.

Therefore, as we have stated previously, this battle cannot be Armageddon. Nor does this battle end in the establishment of the Kingdom of God on earth as does Armageddon.

3. The chaos of nations after the battle of Ezekiel 38-39 will suggest to a war-weary world the need for a single ruler. Out of this chaos the Antichrist will come up strong with a small people and skyrocket to international prominence as the man with the answers.

4. The Antichrist will make a seven-year covenant with Israel, guaranteeing her national security. This security from Arab opposition will be necessary for the rebuilding of the Jewish Temple.

5. The Jerusalem Temple will be built as described in Ezekiel 40-48, which signigicantly follows the story of the destruction of the Russian-led confederation as it attempts to invade Israel. The new Temple is necessary to the Antichrist's later appearance there.

6. The Antichrist will subdue, or reach an agreement with the Arab countries in order to be able to make a valid covenant with Israel. It must be obvious when one considers that there is no way the Jewish Temple can be rebuilt without some concession to Arab sensibilities. Perhaps they will accept a dictated peace: granting permission for Jews to build their Temple in return for guarantees that their oil-rich lands would never again be threatened with invasion. The Antichrist will be in a position to make this guarantee.

These six occurances will alert biblically-informed pople. They will not be deceived into joining the widespread clamor and admiration of unregenerate mankind for the Antichrist. Further, they

should oppose and frustrate him as much as they can
for as long as they can.

What the World Doesn't See

The Antichrist will be revealed to the world after
the restraining influence of the Holy Spirit and the
Christians are removed at the parousia. Believers are
the "salt" of the earth. When the "salt" is removed,
spiritual putrifaction will set in rapidly, and the
Antichrist will soon be revealed to the entire world
for what he is (II Thess. 2:7, 8).

Christians have been much harmed by over simpli-
fied teaching about the Antichrist's unveiling. It has
been falsely supposed that there will be but one
revealing of the man of sin.

However, Scripture describes two revealings. Let
us examine a passage from one of the Apostle Paul's
first written epistles, which states that Christians will
be able to recognize Antichrist before the parousia.

In II Thessalonians, Paul says:

> *"Now we beseech you, brethren, by the
> coming of our Lord Jesus Christ, and by our
> gathering together unto him" (II Thess. 2:1).*

Note "our gathering together unto him" can only
mean the first stage of His second coming when
Christ comes for His own people. In the second
stage, he comes not to "gather" His people, but with
them at Armageddon to finalize the destruction of the
beast and his armies.

The exact event of which St. Paul wrote is the
parousia. See what the Apostle says further about the
Antichrist's coming.

> *"Let no man deceive you by any means: for*

> *that day shall not come, except there come a*
> *falling away first, and that man of sin be*
> *revealed, the son of perdition" (II Thess. 2:3).*

Observe that "the day of the Lord," that part of the "day of the Lord" known as the parousia, will not come until the Antichrist is first revealed!

> *"At the time appointed he shall return, and*
> *come toward the south" (Dan. 11:29).*

> *"He shall stretch forth his hand also upon the*
> *countries; and the land of Egypt shall not*
> *escape. But he shall have power over the trea-*
> *sure of gold and silver, and over all the precious*
> *things of Egypt; and the Libyans and the Ethi-*
> *opians shall be at his steps (be his servants)"*
> *(Dan. 11:43).*

Bible-believing Christians will recognize the Antichrist as such when he makes his covenant with Israel. To the people of the world, this will seem to be an act of statesmanship, peace and good sense. Men will sigh with relief. But Christians will know a time of great trouble will lie ahead. Still, they can rejoice, for soon Christ will appear to gather His own from the four corners of the earth!

CHAPTER 12

The Curtain Falls

So often "wrong" seems eternally on the throne, while "right" is perpetually on the scaffold. This is more apparent than real. Wrong will ultimately fall!

For a time the Antichrist will be so great and powerful that "all the world will wonder after the beast," and will exclaim, "Who is able to make war with him?" (Rev. 13:4). He will be so successful that "all that dwell upon the earth shall worship him, whose names are not in the book of life of the Lamb" (Rev. 13:8).

But his final and swift end is assured, and with his fall comes the end of organized evil in the world! The Antichrist is Satan's last hope. How will his destruction come about?

1. The Antichrist will reign in Jerusalem for three and a half years after having broken a seven-year covenant with Israel halfway through.

"And he shall confirm the covenant with many for one week: and in the midst of the week he

shall cause the sacrifice and the oblation to cease, and for the overspreading of abominations he shall make it desolate, even until the consummation, and that determined shall be poured upon the desolate" (Dan. 9:27).

"And he shall plant the tabernacles of his palace between the seas in the glorious holy mountain; yet he shall come to his end, and none shall help him" (Dan. 11:45).

"And from the time that the daily sacrifice shall be taken away, and the abomination that maketh desolate set up, there shall be a thousand two hundred and ninety days" (Dan. 12:11).

This 1,290 days is the three-and-a-half-year period after he announces that he is the Messiah and ends the recently revived sacrifices in the newly constructed Jewish Temple.

2. His worldwide reign will hardly be under way before God will begin to plague him with great troubles. Consequently, his kingdom will then begin to crumble beneath divine pressure.

"And the fifth angel poured out his vial upon the seat of the beast; and his kingdom was full of darkness; and they gnawed their tongues for pain, And blasphemed the God of heaven because of their deeds" (Rev. 16:10, 11).

"And he shall speak great words against the most High, and shall wear out the saints of the most High, and think to change times and laws: and they shall be given into his hand until a time and times and the dividing of time" (Dan. 7:25).

Again, the three and a half years of his limited

reign are mentioned. The mysterious phrase, "a time and times and the dividing of time," is the equivalent of three and a half years if a "time" means a year, "times" means two years, and "dividing of time" means a half-year.

> *"But the judgment shall sit, and they shall take away his dominion, to consume and to destroy it unto the end" (Dan. 7:26).*

✓ 3. His religious capital (probably Rome, but given the symbolic name of "Babylon"), will then be destroyed. He will first destroy it as a religious center and later God will destroy it completely.

> *"And after these things I saw another angel come down from heaven, having great power; and the earth was lightened with his glory. And he cried mightily with a strong voice, saying, "Babylon the great is fallen, and is become the habitation of devils, and the hold of every foul spirit, and a cage of every unclean and hateful bird. For all nations have drunk of the wine of the wrath of her fornication, and the kings of the earth have committed fornication with her, and the merchants of the earth are waxed rich through the abundance of her delicacies. And I heard another voice from heaven, saying, "Come out of her, my people, that ye be not partaker of her sins, and that ye receive not her plagues. For her sins have reached unto heaven, and God hath remembered her iniquities (Rev. 18:1-5).*

> *"Therefore shall her plagues come in one day, death, and mourning, and famine; and she shall be utterly burned with fire: for strong is the Lord God who judgeth her" (Rev. 18:8).*

> *"Rejoice over her, thou heaven, and ye holy
> apostles and prophets; for God hath avenged
> you on her" (Rev. 18:20).*

> *"And the great city was divided into three
> parts, and the cities of the nations fell: and great
> Babylon came in remembrance before God, to
> give unto her the cup of the wine of the fierceness
> of his wrath" (Rev. 16:19).*

Thus, the kingdom of the Antichrist continues to
disintegrate.

4. As the end approaches, the Antichrist will
organize a military campaign to fight at
Armageddon.

> *"And the sixth angel poured out his vial upon
> the great river Euphrates; and the water thereof
> was dried up, that the way of the kings of the east
> might be prepared. And I saw three unclean
> spirits like frogs come out of the mouth of the
> dragon, and out of the mouth of the beast, and
> out of the mouth of the false prophet. For they
> are the spirits of devils, working miracles, which
> go forth unto the kings of the earth and of the
> whole world, to gather them to the battle of that
> great day of God Almighty . . . And he gathered
> them together into a place called in the Hebrew
> tongue Armageddon" (Rev. 16:12-14, 16).*

Why will the Antichrist presume to fight such a
battle in the first place? Perhaps he will be dazzled by
illusions of his own indestructability, an impression
resulting from his remarkable recovery from a fatal
wound.

There may be another more immediate and
prosaic cause of the gathering of great armies at

Armageddon. Twice the book of The Revelation speaks of the drying of the Euphrates River so that the way of the kings of the East may be prepared. His reference to the Euphrates is probably symbolic of the border between East and West! Perhaps Armageddon at the outset is a struggle between the Orient and the Occident because of famine. At any rate, the first such reference to the involvement of the oriental armies occurs during the seven trumpets:

> *"Saying to the sixth angel which had the trumpet, Loose the four angels which are bound in the great river Euphrates" (Rev. 9:14).*

> *"And the number of the army of the horsemen were two hundred thousand thousand: and I heard the number of them" (Rev. 9:16).*

> *"By these three was the third part of men killed by the fire and by the smoke, and by the brimstone, which issued out of their mouths" (Rev. 9:18).*

The second reference is during the seven vials of judgment:

> *"And the sixth angel poured out his vial upon the great river Euphrates; and the water thereof was dried up, that the way of the kings of the east might be prepared" (Rev. 16:12).*

A curious passage in Daniel also confirms that it is war between the East and West which draws the Antichrist to Armageddon.

> *"But tidings out of the east and out of the north shall trouble him: therefore he shall go forth with great fury to destroy, and utterly to make away many" (Dan. 11:44).*

The "east" may mean the orient, where drought and plagues may have caused famine great enough to provoke the oriental armies (the figure given is 200,000,000 men) to revolt against the Antichrist.

At any rate, whatever the primary cause of Armageddon, the end will be the personal intervention of the armies of God, led by Jesus Christ. At that time, the Antichrist will turn in fury to make war with Him. This action may seem to embody the height of presumption—that the Antichrist would even attempt battle with the Son of God. However, history has proved that dictators have frequently fought hopeless battles in the self-delusion of their paranoia. Hitler is the most recent case in point.

> *"And I saw the beast, and the kings of the earth, and their armies, gathered together to make war against him that sat on the horse, and against his army" (Rev. 19:19).*

5. The power of the Antichrist will then be utterly shattered.

> *"And then shall that Wicked be revealed, whom the Lord shall consume with the spirit of his mouth, and shall destroy with the brightness of his coming" (II Thess. 2:8).*

6. The details of the Battle of Armageddon are told by John:

> *"And I saw heaven opened, and behold a white horse: and he that sat upon him was called Faithful and True, and in righteousness he doth judge and make war. His eyes were as a flame of fire, and on his head were many crowns; and he had a name written, that no man knew, but he*

*himself. And he was clothed with a vesture
dipped in blood: and his name is called The
Word of God. And the armies which were in
heaven followed him upon white horses, clothed
in fine linen, white and clean. And out of his
mouth goeth a sharp sword, that with it he
should smite the nations: and he shall rule them
with a rod of iron: and he treadeth the winepress
of the fierceness and wrath of Almighty God.
And he hath on his vesture and on his thigh a
name written, KING OF KINGS, AND LORD
OF LORDS. And I saw an angel standing in the
sun; and he cried with a loud voice, saying to all
the fowls that fly in the midst of heaven, Come
and gather yourselves together unto the supper
of the great God, That we may eat the flesh of
kings, and the flesh of captains, and the flesh of
mighty men, and the flesh of horses, and of
them that sit on them, and the flesh of all men,
both free and bond, both small and great" (Rev.
19:11-18).*

7. The battle will culminate in the judgment of
Antichrist who will be cast into the final (second) hell
with Satan.

*"And the beast was taken, and with him the
false prophet that wrought miracles before him,
with which he deceived them that had received
the mark of the beast, and them that worshipped
his image. These both were cast alive into a lake
of fire burning with brimstone" (Rev. 19:20).*

*"And the devil that deceived them was cast
into the lake of fire and brimstone, where the
beast and the false prophet are, and shall be*

tormented day and night for ever and ever"
(Rev. 20:10).

8. All those who fought with the beast shall also be destroyed.

"And the remnant were slain with the sword of
him that sat upon the horse, which sword
proceeded out of his mouth: and all the fowls
were filled with their flesh" (Rev. 19:21).

9. God's people will be at last delivered, rewarded and vindicated. They will then reign with Christ for a thousand years.

"And I saw thrones, and they sat upon them,
and judgment was given unto them; and I saw
the souls of them that were beheaded for the
witness of Jesus, and for the word of God, and
which had not worshipped the beast, neither his
image, neither had received his mark upon their
foreheads, or in their hands; and they lived and
reigned with Christ a thousand years" (Rev.
20:4).

Thus will end the career of the most powerful human who has ever lived. It is possible that he is on earth today. Perhaps he has already made his covenant with Satan and is on the rise. Before long, Bible-taught Christians may be able to recognize him. When that occurs, the return of Jesus Christ will surely not be long in coming!

the terrible one

Appendix 1

Biblical Names and References to the Antichrist

In the Old Testament, at least twenty-five names may refer to the Antichrist:

the bloody and deceitful man.......................(Ps.5:6)
the wicked one..(Ps. 10:2-4)
the man of the earth...............................(Ps. 10:18)
the mighty man.......................................(Ps. 52:1)
the enemy...(Ps. 55:3)
the adversary..(Ps 74:8-10)
the head over many countries..................(Ps. 110:6)
the violent man..... ....(Ps. 140:1)
the Assyrian.................................(Isa. 16:4, 5, 12)
the King of Babylon.................................(Isa. 14:4)
the spoiler...........................(Isa. 16:4, 5; Jer. 6:26)
the nail...(Isa. 22:25)
the branch of the terrible ones...................(Isa. 25:5)
the profane and wicked
prince of Israel..............................(Ezek. 21:25-27)
the little horn...(Dan. 7:8)
the prince that shall come.......................(Dan. 9:26)
the vile person.....................................(Dan. 11:21)
the willful king.....................................(Dan. 11:36)

the idol shepherd............................(Zech. 11:16, 17)
"the man that shall die".........................(Isa. 51:12)
"the terrible one"...................................(Isa. 29:30)
"thy seed" (of the serpent).....................(Gen. 3:15)

In the New Testament, eight names or titles are given to the Antichrist:
"the abomination of desolation".........(Matt. 24:15)
"the false Christ"................................(Matt. 24:24)
"another (who) shall come in
his own name..(John 5:43)
"that man of sin" (better translated as "the lawless one" and as
"the son of perdition".........................(II Thess. 2:3)
Antichrist.............................(I John 2:18; II John 7)
"Beast"..(Rev. 11:7; 13:2)

Appendix 2

Many scholars have tried to chart the divine plans of both history and prophecy. None have fully succeeded and we disavow dogmatism in this attempt.

History is searched to discover the patterns of the past; prophecy is consulted to determine the patterns of the future. Some attempts of this type of study have been useful, but most have suffered from three grave errors: (1) over-simplification; (2) making local or provincial events assume universal meanings ; and (3) ignoring Scriptural passages which disagree with the charts. Much prophetic fulfillment is plain today which was not understood even a generation ago. Thus, the old charts tend to be incomplete or erroneous.

Perhaps we should consider that the main error of charting the book of The Revelation is that of using the twenty-one great events of that book as a continuously developing pattern of the future. We refer to the events pictured by the "seven seals," the "seven trumpets" and "seven bowls," and it is natural, perhaps, to assume that there are twenty-one consecutive events so listed. But could there be another explanation?

We suggest that we fix our pattern of future things upon other events which, beyond argument, will happen. Rather than work forward through the three "sevens," let us work backwards from the other events which are firmly established by plain Scriptural statements of time, fact and relationship.

This may give us a clearer picture of the plan of the future. The twenty-one events of the book of The Revelation can then be fitted into a secondary pattern and fall into place where they possibly or probably belong.

The resurrection and translation of Christians (i.e., catching up of living and dead at the first stage of Christ's second coming) is here assumed to occur at the conjunction of the events of the seventh seal and the seventh trumpet, which we believe to be the same or a parallel series of events: the seals from earth's point of view, the trumpets from God's point of view.

The three-and-a-half-year time intervals (see chart) are all plainly stated in Scripture. The Antichrist reigns supreme for only three and a half years (Rev. 13:5), after he appears blasphemously in the new Jewish Temple. The Temple cannot be built before the Russian invasion of Israel, and yet it must be completed by the time the sacrifices begin and the Antichrist appears to cause sacrifices to cease.

The clearing of the debris of the Russian invasion takes seven years (Ezek. 39:9). The Antichrist is to sign a seven-year covenant of protection of Israel and is to break it halfway through this period. When he breaks the covenant, it has existed only three and a half years. When he does so, he has three and a half years left to rule. Therefore, the covenant is signed seven years before Armageddon. Put these facts all together and then the periods of three and a half years each make a consistent plan.

Keep in mind that Israel cannot begin to build the Temple before the covenant with the Antichrist, nor can the construction start until three and a half years before the Antichrist enters the Temple. Hence, the building of the Temple will take three and a half years (which is reasonable for so great and important a building) from the time the covenant is made with the Antichrist.

The Antichrist does not appear at the battle of Ezekiel 38-39, and there are to be, as we have noted, seven years before the debris is completely removed. Hence, the earliest the Antichrist can rise to power after that Russian-led invasion, and be strong enough to insure Israel to have permission from the Arabs to build after the demolition of the Dome of the Rock, the Moslem temple now standing on the site where the Jews' Temple is to be built, will be three and a half years (the first period on the chart) after the Russian invasion attempt. This explanation allows a reasonable time for all these events to take place. Hence, the three periods of three and a half years are each anchored to a definite Scriptural time.

The "Tribulation," consisting of the simultaneous appearing of the seven seals and the seven trumpets, begins at the time of the signing of the covenant between the Antichrist and Israel. It ends with the seventh seal and the seventh trumpet (i.e., "the last trumpet," I Cor. 15:52) at which time Christ returns for His own and the first resurrection occurs.

Immediately thereafter, Satan is forever expelled from Heaven (Rev. 12:9), and the Antichrist, previously revealed to Christians (II Thess. 2:1, 2), is now revealed to the world as its "messiah." Thus there are two "revealings" of the Antichrist, differentiated by Paul in II Thessalonians 2:7-8. The "Great Tribulation" then begins and lasts three and a half years until Armageddon.

The battle of Ezekiel 38-39 is certainly not Armageddon. At Armageddon there is total destruction of the enemies of God, but at the end of the northern confederacy's invasion only five-sixths of the army is destroyed. Armageddon is fought at Megiddo in Israel, while the battle with Russia is fought in a valley east of the sea (Ezek. 39:11).

At the time of the Battle of Armageddon, the Antichrist has already profaned the Temple for three and a half years. At the time of the Russian invasion, no Temple exists, but is built afterwards. Ezekiel 40 tells of this in the logical sequence in which the fortieth chapter follows after the thirty-ninth chapter, which tells of the destruction of the Russian army.

Remember, chapter divisions did not exist in Ezekiel's day, and the events of chapters 38-39 are followed logically by the events of chapters 40-48. Since a Temple must be built before the Antichrist enters it, it can obviously only be built after the events of Ezekiel 38-39. The old explanation that the Temple of Ezekiel 40-48 is the millennial Temple will not do. No other Scripture passage confirms it. In any case, there is no reason why this temple cannot be cleansed and reused in the millennium. The order of these events is clear on the chart.

BEGINNING OF THE END OF
THIS PRESENT AGE

(Luke 21:25) Signs of fulfillment of Biblical prophecy appear.

Israel regathers (Isa. 11:11-12).

The Apostasy Begins (II Thess. 2:1-2). The sentiment for a one-world government appears.

The Apostate, worldwide, universalist and ecumenical movements are born, laying the foundations of apostate and pagan "Babylon."

The Nuclear Age begins, with Apocalyptic overtones.

Distress of nations.

Signs in the sun and moon.

The "times of the Gentiles"—rule in Jerusalem ends (1967).

Communications and transportation technology opens the way for world government.

The antichrist is born.

Atheistic communism seeks world domination via single party rule.

SUDDEN GREAT EVENT—THE RUSSIAN
CONFEDERACY INVADES ISRAEL

(Ezek. 38-39) The war is between Communist countries of Eastern Europe and Israel, certain Arabs, the Atlantic nations and their colonies or ex-colonies.

The Russian aim is to seize the strategic land and

waterways of the Middle East now under Israeli control, and to "take a spoil," probably the control of Middle Eastern oil reserves.

Battle to be fought in section of Israel east of the Sea of Galilee. Five-sixths of the northern army destroyed by fire. Northern homelands hurt by fire-storms (nuclear?)

Russian "empire" fragmented and power partially destroyed. Israel delivered—Jerusalem untouched.

War followed by burial of dead, burning of weapons, graves in the valley of Hamon-gog. This takes seven years.

EMERGENCE OF THE ANTICHRIST— 3½ YEARS

(Dan. 8:25) International chaos.

Realignment of nations.

Rise of Antichrist (not present in the war of Ezekiel 38-39), first with a small people, then a ten-nation confederacy. Antichrist to come from one of the divisions of Alexander's empire (which included part of what is now the Soviet Union).

Antichrist comes to power by deceit, false "peace," war, threats of war and socialism (see Dan. 11:24).

He is hailed as the man with the answers.

He will deceive many.

He rises to great power in three-and-a-half years.

The opening of the seven seals. (Rev. 6:2)

148

THE "TRIBULATIOIN" - 3½ YEARS

(Dan. 9:27) Begins with Antichrist signing seven-year covenant with Israel, which opens the way for Israel to construct a temple and begin sacrifices by the end of three-and-a-half years.

Antichrist is thus identified by Christians though he is unrecognized as such by the rest of mankind (see II Thess. 2:1-2).

The beginning of world rule by the Antichrist.

The rapid rise of a world pagan and apostate religious organization with government recognition in Rome.

Daniel's Seventieth "week" begins.

The judgment of the seven trumpets (Rev. 8:2).

SUDDEN GREAT EVENT—THE SECOND COMING OF CHRIST (first-stage resurrection)

(I Thess. 4:13-17, I Cor. 15:51-57, Rev. 11:15-18) Christ comes for His own people and to raise the godly dead.

Heaven is silent at the time of the seventh seal.

This is the first resurrection. Those who have life eternal and are still alive on earth are caught up into the clouds for a reunion, and for the judgment of the believer's earthly service, at the "Bema" or judgment seat.

The Resurrection body is bestowed.

Works tested by fire. All true Christians have disappeared from earth.

Holy Spirit and churches cease to hinder or restrain Antichrist.

THE "GREAT TRIBULATION" - 3½ YEARS

(Dan. 9:24) Satan banished from Heaven forever. The "Accuser" is cast down to earth in great wrath because he knows he has but a short time (see Rev. 12:9).

Antichrist revealed to the world.

Antichrist stops worship in Jerusalem temple, proclaims himself the "messiah" and demands worship.

He reigns in Jerusalem for three-and-a-half years (see Rev. 11:12, Dan. 9:27, Dan. 11:45).

Godly remnant of Israel refuses worship, flees to Jordanian wilderness (Petra?).

Martydom for those who refuse Antichrist's mark or worship.

Great judgments of God poured out upon Antichrist's kingdom.

This is the period of the "seven bowl judgments."

The Antichrist is revealed (by blasphemy in the Temple) to the world.

SUDDEN GREAT EVENT— ARMAGEDDON

(Rev. 14:14, Rev. 16:19, Rev. 19:17) Spirits from the Antichrist, the False Prophet and Satan are sent to gather the nations to the Battle of Armageggon, to be located in the valley of Megiddo near Nazareth.

The armies of God (angels and saints with Jesus

Christ at their head) defeat this confederacy o:
godless world government.

Antichrist and false prophet cast into lake of fire and
Satan is bound for one thousand years in the
"bottomless pit."

Rebel armies slain.

All war and rebellion cease for one thousand years.

MILLENIAL REIGN—1000 YEARS

(Rev. 20:4) Kindgom of God on earth.

Jesus Christ rules all nations from Jerusalem.

Universal peace and justice.

Animals live peaceably.

Saints rule with Christ and judge mankind.

People of earth frequently go to Jerusalem to wor
ship, many once each year.

Life lengthens, death recedes.

All dwell safely; no Satan opposes them.

Temple is cleansed and reused.

Justice prevails

No wars.

SUDDEN GREAT EVENT—
LAST REBELLION

(Rev. 20:7) Satan is loosed to tempt those born in th
millenium.

Brief rebellion occurs, known as the second Battle of Gog and Magog.

Fire comes down upon the rebel army as it surrounds Jerusalem, and destroys it.

Satan is cast forever into lake of fire (Rev. 20:10).

Then occurs the final judgment of all mankind apart from Christians who appear only as witnesses.

Books are opened. Purpose of judgment is to justify God's justice.

Those not found in Lamb's Book of Life cast into lake of fire.

Earth destroyed, melted by fire. (II Peter 3:11)

THE NEW THINGS ON THE NEW EARTH

(Rev. 21:1-2; 2:19)

Seven New Things: New Earth; New Heaven; New City; New Center of World; New Temple; New Healing; New Light; New Task

Seven Things Which Will Not Appear: No Death, No Night, No Sin, No Lies, No Unpleasant Memories of Earthly Existence, No Rebels, No Sickness.